DELHI UNIVERSITY

DELHI UNIVERSITY

Celebrating 100 Glorious Years

Edited by

HARDEEP S. PURI

RUPA

First published by
Rupa Publications India Pvt. Ltd 2022
7/16, Ansari Road, Daryaganj
New Delhi 110002

Sales Centres:

Allahabad Bengaluru Chennai
Hyderabad Jaipur Kathmandu
Kolkata Mumbai

ISBN: 978-93-5520-388-5

First impression 2022

10 9 8 7 6 5 4 3 2 1

Printed in India

CONTENTS

Foreword by Amitabh Bachchan vii

Editor's Note xiii

1. From the Desk of a Former VC 1
   Dinesh Singh

2. Journey of a Hundred Years 14
   Sanjeev Sanyal

3. Remembering DU via Stephania 32
   Shashi Tharoor

4. A Tryst with Economics and Law 46
   Dhananjaya Y. Chandrachud

5. Dakshinamurty: Notes from the South and Feminist Legacy 54
   Lakshmi Puri

6. Of Buses, Theatrics and a Disobedient Spirit 74
   Imtiaz Ali

7. Leading and Learning from the Churn 84
   Arnab Goswami

8. The Best Days of My Life 91
Raian Karanjawala

9. An Island Called D-School 106
Bibek Debroy

10. Hervoice@DU.100: Engendering the Academy 122
Meenakshi Gopinath

11. Integration and Aspiration 145
Kiren Rijiju

12. Trials, Travails and Triumphs at JMC 149
Namita Gokhale

13. The Start of Starting Up 157
Vijay Shekhar Sharma

14. The Three Defining Conflicts That Shaped My Life 166
Hardeep S. Puri

About the Contributors 188

FOREWORD

When the Honourable Shri Hardeep S. Puri wrote to me about his plans to publish an anthology to celebrate the centenary of Delhi University and invited me as a celebrated alumnus to write a few words on this magnificent occasion, I wrote back and told him that I was the wrong person to be asked to do this.

I did not believe that I fell into the category of 'eminent personalities' he had given reference to, as my years at the university (1958–61) were an academic embarrassment to me. If I were to write something, it would all be rather frivolous and not in keeping with the grace and intent of the anthology, I told him. But he persisted, and I relented.

The DU (North Campus) where I sought admission and studied was, perhaps, patterned along the lines of the Cambridge and Oxford universities in the United Kingdom (UK), where several colleges stood side by side at one prominent location, many sharing common boundaries—not just of the physical built environment but also of a deeper educative ethos of imparting the requisite attitudes, values and knowledge to build generations of leaders.

This shared situatedness imbued immense camaraderie among the students. We would stroll into each other's colleges, mix with fellow students, relax at each other's canteens, travel in the same university bus to our home locations, become bitter rivals at intercollegiate competitions, and immediately forget all that animosity to join our voices in cheering for the university when it played against another.

This was 1958, and I was at Kirori Mal College pursuing the BSc General course, from which I just about graduated in my final year. Academically, it was the wrong decision to take up Science, but the years spent there were an education in many other spheres, which has proved to be invaluable in my life. Looking back at the influence of my education on my career, I realize that it is the amalgamation of diverse disciplines that inspires every form of creative activity. For instance, where would writers be without a printing press, stage thespians without a proscenium and lights, painters without pigments and canvas, and, in my case, film actors without a camera? Education engenders myriad symbiotic opportunities in the spheres of technology and humanities.

Chances are very high that I would not have been in cinema or in any other creative aspect of life without a grounding in education—education which is in consonance with the belief that 'what sculpture is to a block of marble, education is to the human soul'. Before leaving the hallowed grounds of university, we sculpt our identity; we strengthen and fortify our convictions in a manner that we do not fall into a trap—the trap of being swayed by the prejudices of caste and creed, and race and religion.

During my days at the university, classes were held at the main university building, while the subsidiaries and practicals were conducted at the various individual colleges. It goes without saying that there is a palpable nostalgia as I think back on the hours spent at the Coffee House, or at the bus stop outside Miranda House (yes, always outside Miranda House), or on the sports field that would host intercollegiate and inter-university cricket matches, and, of course, in the classroom where regular attendance paid its dividends when it came to term-end examinations.

If I may be permitted to stroll down memory lane a little more, it was at DU that I received my first serious encouragement as an actor. The tall and imposing Mr Frank Thakurdas of the dramatics club paid me my first compliment when I performed in a stage production of Maxwell Anderson's *Winterset*. He recommended me to the USIS drama company to play the part of Abraham Lincoln, and chose me for the part of Zeus in Benn Levy's *The Rape of the Belt*, staged at Miranda House.

Mr Thakurdas remains a part of me. So does Dr Swaroop Singh, a messianic educationist who was the principal of Kirori Mal when I was studying there and later became the university's vice chancellor. Without saying it in so many words, he made us realize that we needn't aspire towards a graduation degree merely because of peer or parental pressure. He reminded us that we should aspire to become graduates because we feel the desire to be complete with the advantage of formal education.

For argument's sake, some may opine today that education isn't mandatory any more, with the proliferation of what some may call 'unconventional' jobs and vocations. Some may wonder about the relevance of a degree if one cannot apply it later in one's profession. To my mind, these arguments are superfluous. To be sure, it is a bonus if we can use our education directly in our everyday work—in fact, that would be ideal. However, even if that weren't to be the case, the years spent on campus serve a much more vital purpose—they broaden our knowledge about the world around us, besides aiding personality development.

Clearly, initiative in reading at the library, participating in cultural events, and asking more of ourselves and of our educationists, add up to making us aware and concerned citizens. As the proverb goes: Whatever is good to know is difficult to learn.

Moreover, no one can argue against the fact that campus life is the formative stage in every individual's life; that is when we 'remove the shackles', as it were. Suddenly, from a regimented life, we are free to make our decisions and heuristically zero in on the subject we want to study or the vocation we want to take up. It is a key period in any young person's life—one of choice. My father taught English and poetry, and he expected me to opt for Arts in college. When I didn't, he was accommodative and understanding.

Certainly, the youth of today—in fact, of any day and age—does not want to be preached at. As time goes by, they become more clued-up and more aware of their needs and aspirations. They can see which route to take on the highway of the future. But, believe me, that is not enough. They must also know their speed limits, when to turn and when to apply the brakes. The University of Delhi was absolutely essential in that regard.

Time sped its way along, and then one fine day, almost 50 years after I joined Kirori Mal, I was informed that Delhi University was decorating me with an honorary doctorate. The first sentiment was to express my limitless gratitude. Who would have thought that an ordinary student graduate would someday be accorded such an overwhelming homecoming?

My immediate response after that was to ask myself if I deserved an honour of such magnitude. Was I worthy to be honoured by my university, my very own family, which gave me some of the most wonderful years of my life? This was the same institution that inculcated in me the values and principles of life that I cherish deeply and will abide by to my dying day. Among all the accolades that I have been extremely fortunate to have received, it is, perhaps ironically, being bestowed with this honorary doctorate that I regard as one of the highest honours.

A lifelong debt is owed to the University of Delhi. I feel it is only fair that I reciprocate the tremendous faith and honour the university has shown me. This anthology, edited by Shri Hardeep S. Puri ji and including some fascinating entries by other more deserving alumni of the DU family, allows me to pay my respects. Indeed, it was a privilege to be at the nation's premier seat of learning—one which has always championed the cause of education since its inception a hundred years ago.

My best wishes to the University of Delhi.

In gratitude,
Amitabh Bachchan

EDITOR'S NOTE

A hundred years is an important milestone in the life of any institution. The centenary of a university becomes all the more important because centres of learning, particularly those that aspire to excellence, need to compete with universities that have quite literally been hundreds of years in existence.

Equally, to be included in any list of alumni invited to contribute to this anthology on the occasion of 100 years of Delhi University is, in and of itself, a singular honour. Without doubt, those who have been invited to contribute are eminently qualified in several respects: they have made a name for themselves in their chosen profession; by and large, they have made a positive contribution not only to their profession but also to the larger public cause; and, whilst one may or may not agree with the political views they espouse or the trajectory that they may have embarked upon, they do stand out.

Clearly, in an exercise like this, those who would appear to qualify far exceeds the number that even an extended anthology can accommodate. Also, not everybody invited has the time or the inclination to join the list of contributors. When I was invited to coordinate this effort, my immediate preoccupation was to put together a list of interesting people, successful professionals and particularly those who would avoid the temptation of utilizing this as an opportunity to blow their own trumpet. Instead, based on their personal and anecdotal experience, I hoped they would provide insights into how they benefitted from this great institution and how, in turn, they shaped the outcome of their interaction with their immediate environment in the university. Are those lessons cherished by the contributor? Do they provide a possible template for others entering the university now?

These and several other thoughts crossed my mind when I was approached by Rupa Publications to draw up a list of contributors. It did not strike me then that this would be somewhat time-consuming and that my duties as a member of the Cabinet and involvement in other political activities may prove limiting. Assisted by an able researcher who has the potential of becoming an outstanding wordsmith, Rohit Saxena, as well as the support from Kapish Mehra and Yamini Chowdhury at Rupa Publications, this became both an interesting and educative exercise. I also would like to thank Child Rights and You (CRY), a renowned non-profit organization, which partnered with us on this anthology. All the proceeds from the sales of this anthology will go towards strengthening their exemplary work on child rights and education.

The individuals invited to contribute to this anthology comprise, in a sense, a list of celebrities—the who's who of their professions. I am extremely grateful for the time they have given to their chapters, especially given their busy schedules. Ultimately, it is they who must take the credit for this anthology. Some contributors went above and beyond, and came back to me with the most amazing nugget of detail or memory that added a new dimension to a chapter, or even the anthology. Keeping in mind that this book is a celebration of the university completing 100 years, it was important that the contributors wrote with a light touch that focused more on their personal experiences rather than academic detail. Within that remit, however, I was pleasantly surprised to find that the contributors sent entries of the highest calibre and scholarly attention—viewed together, they encapsulate the eclectic diversity of the university.

I was honoured that Amitabh Bachchan agreed to write the Foreword. The oldest alumnus in this list, he is also the most revered. A doyen of the Indian film industry and ambassador for India's artistic excellence, he is a national treasure who is recognized across the world. His disarmingly humble recollections of his time at Kirori Mal College provide warmth and familiarity, even as he passes on some profound messages for readers and alumni alike.

It was pleasing to receive an introspective chapter from the Honourable Dr Justice Dhananjaya Y. Chandrachud. While describing his time studying at St. Stephen's College and Faculty of Law, in two different disciplines, he makes a compelling case for the quality of education at DU. His remarks on the interdisciplinary nature of the pedagogy and the university's emphasis on teaching students how to think rather than merely learn are highly relevant.

My colleague in the Cabinet, Kiren Rijiju, the minister of law and justice, has written a noteworthy message on how studying at Hansraj College and absorbing the shared experience of DU helped expand his horizons. Kiren's focus on the central role that the university has played in integrating the Northeast within the larger conceptions of India is succinct and stirring, drawing attention to the potential that educational institutions have in furthering plurality.

Dr Shashi Tharoor's chapter contains all the characteristic flair and poise that one has come to associate with him. However, underneath the humorous refrains and anecdotes from his undergraduate days, Shashi conveys an unmistakeable affection and gratitude for St. Stephen's that is worth perusing.

I was glad that Prof. (Dr) Dinesh Singh agreed to contribute a chapter. As a former vice chancellor of the university between 2010 and 2015, he has a unique vantage point. His reflections combine the experiences of not just an executive authority who helped modernize the institution and incubate innovative educational projects but also a student of the university who went on to become one of India's most distinguished mathematicians.

When I called Dr Bibek Debroy to invite him to write for this anthology, I was pleasantly surprised that he turned around an engaging piece in no time at all. In hindsight, I shouldn't have been surprised. After all, he is among India's most-respected public intellectuals and an economist par excellence—no wonder that he would write with such witty cadence about his time at the Delhi School of Economics (DSE).

Dr Meenakshi Gopinath is one of India's leading educationalists and feminist thinkers. It was particularly satisfying to receive a scholarly account of the engendering of higher secondary education in India as well as DU's instrumental role in the cause. As a beloved principal of Lady Shri Ram College (LSR) for Women, Dr Gopinath provides an administrator's perspective on the evolution of not just the college but also the university.

I was pleased to receive a chapter on the history of the university from the multitalented Sanjeev Sanyal. A young leader who has seen success in various knowledge disciplines through both action and ideas, Sanjeev is part of a rare group of public intellectuals in the country who significantly impact policy and discourse. In weaving a highly readable narrative on the history of the university, Sanjeev beautifully captures the enduring impact of DU.

I was delighted to receive a thought-provoking rumination from Lakshmi M. Puri. Even though we studied at the same time, the distance between the North and South campuses meant that we never met until after we had graduated. As my soulmate and companion for life, I have observed Lakshmi at close quarters for more than 48 years now. I relate with her deep fondness towards the transformative role of the university in our lives. I am sure the reader will join me in marvelling at the way she has intertwined her later journey as a diplomat and gender equality advocate with her intellectual awakenings at LSR.

Raian Karanjawala is not only among India's foremost legal strategists but also a dear friend who accepted my invitation without a moment's hesitation. He reflects on the various sociopolitical goings-on at the Shri Ram College of Commerce (SRCC) and DU in the early 1970s. Within the personal recollection, Raian includes moments of deep significance that convey the sense of turbulence and change that the university was going through at the time.

Namita Gokhale has written a beautifully complex account of her time at the university. The story of why she could not finish her undergraduate degree at Jesus and Mary College (JMC) is utterly fascinating—to use her words, 'troubled but rewarding'. One of India's leading novelists and littérateurs, her typically sharp writing comes through in the most charming of ways as she describes her trials and travails at the university, including her plunge into writing and publishing.

Vijay Shekhar Sharma is perhaps the most well-known entrepreneur in the country—he is a symbol of the new India that is capitalizing on its abundant capacity for disruptive thinking and innovation. He has contributed an inspirational piece, reminding us all of the university's inclusive and vibrant spirit that allows everyone to thrive. His message will resonate with many students and alumni who live under the misguided notion that DU is an elite space.

I am grateful to Imtiaz Ali who has written an amusing account of his time at the university. A junior from my alma mater, he holds a special place in the pantheon of Hindu College alumni. He founded Ibtida, perhaps the most famous Hindi dramatics society in the Delhi circuit. Many readers, and especially DU alumni, will reconnect with the 'disobedient spirit' that he refers to, even as they remember their college days through Imtiaz's evocative writing.

Lastly, I was glad to have received a characteristically opinionated and heart-warming message from Arnab Goswami just as I was about to begin compiling the anthology. His is among the most sought-after and recognized voices in the country, and it was important to me that his unique insight be added to the anthology. Many readers will undoubtedly relate with his personal journey that reveals a story of tenacity, ambition and success.

◆

This anthology has brought in a spectrum of viewpoints that covers five decades of studying or teaching at various colleges in DU, from the late 1950s to the late 1990s. To the extent possible, these contributors also cover the length and breadth of the country—not just geographically but also in terms of the cultures, experiences and professions they represent. No compilation can be exhaustive, especially one such as this, which only puts forth the perspective of 15 alumni of an institution that has seen millions pass through its gates. However, what became clear to me as I was editing individual pieces was that the contributors from both humble, rural beginnings as well as those with elite, urban upbringing have written about their growth at DU with surprisingly similar sentiment. There is an unsaid realization that, in the midst of this mighty institution of learning, something much larger than circumstance connects us all.

All the contributors have touched upon the legacy of the institution and have tried to convey the gravity of the university through their reflections. I would like to use this opportunity to add a few words on the subject. As with most other alumni, there is a confluence of emotions when I think about the university today. Mixed with the flooding of happy memories is a tinge of nostalgia for a familial love towards the institution and its nourishing milieu. There is an eternal bond—a feeling I share with fellow alumni and students of the university.

As the university reached the landmark of 100 years in May 2022, there were discussions held on the significance of the institution and what it has meant for the Indian educational ecosystem. To my mind, it is indisputable that the university has had a central influence on India's growth as well as its mission of producing young and dynamic leaders. The evolution of the university mirrors the journey of Delhi in many ways—together, they have both assumed dominance in Indian intellectual and public life.

Some might argue that such questions of legacy are mammoth undertakings that suggest themselves to serious academic formulation. While I do not disagree—and, in fact, look forward to increased historical discourse on the significance of DU—I seek to use my own memories of the institution in making a humble attempt at describing the university's intangible impact on my life. I believe that in personal stories such as mine and those of the contributors in this anthology, there lies a truer estimation of the enormous influence of the university than in any purposive narrative.

Aggregating personal stories can be an exercise akin to understanding the whole as the sum of its parts. In this case, individual stories of growth, agency, empowerment, mobility and prosperity are appropriate means to consider the university's influence. This is what this anthology seeks to do. However, one also recognizes that an institution grows and morphs to become an entirely new creation that is much more than a simple dynamic of its constituent components. In that regard, no anthology, or for the matter even academic discourse could ever encapsulate the complete legacy of the University of Delhi. Language is too blunt an instrument to do justice to lived experience, too reductive to quantify heritage and too distant to capture feeling.

For every student, it is invariably the indescribable feeling associated with those personal experiences that separates the university from being a mere brick-and-mortar constellation to being an anchor of extreme significance in their lives. And that is what I hope the readers will experience and remember once again as they read this anthology.

It is to the University of Delhi and its students that I dedicate this anthology.

FROM THE DESK OF A FORMER VC

Dinesh Singh

Over time, my association with Delhi University has acquired many hues and tones, which I cherish with a fondness that increases with the passage of time. Of course, the duration of this bond has also necessarily had to grow. However, and more interestingly, in this, the centenary year of the birth of my 'nourishing mother'—or alma mater in more formal terms—this connect has matured into exactly half the hundred-year lifespan of the venerable university. And as the years roll by, this association—like a good burgundy—shall be that much more cherished.

My late father, U.N. Singh, who helped helm this venerable institution in earlier times, often used to aver that there is a bewitching quality about it that invariably casts a spell on those who have come to be touched by it. I, personally, have witnessed, over these decades, some famous and some not-so-well-known names alike that have been embraced by its magic. Incidentally, my father was as much a fan as anyone. After all, he and I have had the privilege—at different times—of according our seal and signatures to the formal degrees of their offspring. This is the only time it has happened in the history of DU. Somewhere in that list of its eternal fans, my name, too, lurks in blissful existence, and here is my chance to convey my gratitude for the blessings showered on me by the university. I, thus, offer this quasi-historical perspective as much as an ode as also an account of some fascinating aspects of the journey of the university.

In 2015, during my stewardship of the university, we produced a delightful and highly lauded *son et lumière* (sound and light) show depicting the history of DU. It was entitled 'University of Delhi: A Legend'. The production values of this show were indeed extraordinary. I say this as a means of offering tribute to the strength and vision that reside within this venerable institution, as the show and its production had succeeded in creating history of sorts. As far as I can tell, such a show has been a one-of-its-kind amongst universities of the world; certainly, a first for an Indian university.

The narrative, as proffered by it, provided a scintillating insight into the hallowed origins of DU and how the journey of the university has been entwined with the destiny of modern India. Just what are these hallowed underpinnings? Let me commence my version of the story by recounting the connections and contributions of DU to India's freedom struggle.

It is worth noting, first and foremost, that the so-called old Viceregal Lodge, which houses the office of the vice chancellor and his team, has served as the official residence of five viceroys of British India. Lord Irwin was the last of these five to have resided there and was also the first occupant in the new Viceregal Lodge that is now known as Rashtrapati Bhavan. Mahatma Gandhi visited Irwin in both these dwellings to parley.

Sometime before I assumed office, I had become aware that an underground dungeon of sorts existed in this building that had housed—in secret and at different times—the three great freedom fighters Rash Behari Bose, Bhagat Singh and Aruna Asaf Ali. Upon trying to locate the cell, I was disappointed and even saddened to see that it had become a sort of dump for what looked like unwanted artefacts and trash accumulated by the university over the decades. Restoring the dungeon took some imaginative effort, and we recreated somewhat the conditions of the cell that had housed Bhagat Singh in that gaol. The benefits on the side that descended from this effort included the discovery of some interesting objects, including what may perhaps have been the first official seal of the university.

This old Viceregal Lodge started out as a hunting lodge that was in existence in 1857. When the British were evicted from Delhi during the early days of the Great Uprising, they sought refuge on the ridge near the lodge and particularly around the flagstaff that stands till today. The revolutionaries had surrounded the firangis on the ridge but tarried for a couple of days on the lower reaches of the ridge, before launching an assault. The delay bought valuable time for reinforcements to arrive from Nepal, and this proved fatal for the revolutionaries. Some of the fiercest battles of 1857 took place on this hallowed ground. The university stands blessed by the sacrifices of those revolutionaries. When the capital shifted from Calcutta to Delhi, the hunting lodge was enlarged and enhanced to a status befitting the official residence of a viceroy.

The saga of the university's own contribution to India's freedom struggle gained momentum over time, but I would like to believe that the sacrifices of our martyrs on the ridge spurred them. The university shifted from Kashmere Gate—where it was housed in a building that subsequently gave way to the now erstwhile Ritz Cinema—and moved to its present environs in the 1930s. It had also matured, by then, from a purely examining body into a full-fledged teaching and research institution.

What many of us may be unaware of is that Gandhiji had a very intimate connection with DU through St. Stephen's College, which is one of its three founding colleges. The draft of Gandhiji's first non-cooperation call to India was prepared at the residence of the then principal of St. Stephen's, Sushil Kumar Rudra. It was finalized with the assistance of Rudra and the redoubtable Charles Freer Andrews, the vice principal of the college. Gandhiji had also exhorted Rudra's students to give up their studies and actively participate in his movement. The British frowned upon Gandhiji's visits and brought pressure to bear on Rudra to prevent Gandhiji's presence on campus. Rudra's fearless and firm response is worthy of recounting. He was quick to assert to the powers that were by averring that he was a Christian whose doors were open to all, and most of all, for Gandhiji. Hindu College also played a memorable role in the freedom struggle. Chandrashekhar Azad sought refuge in the hostel of Hindu College with the assistance of the warden. Soon thereafter, Azad barely managed to dodge a police raid having been betrayed by someone's treachery. The warden had to subsequently pay a heavy price.

Thinker, Reformer, Implementer

The university turned a major corner and donned (pun intended) the mantle of a leading seat of knowledge and learning in 1938 when Sir Maurice Gwyer assumed the office of vice chancellor. In this context, some things are worthy of mention. Gwyer had no major academic credentials to his credit, and for a substantial period, he also doubled up in the role of the Chief Justice of India. Yet, his stewardship of DU anoints him as one of our finest vice chancellors. He served for three consecutive terms of four years each, and this continuity enabled him to bring about far-reaching changes and reforms. Of course, he also had the required vision and acumen to carry out his ideas. There are several learnings to be derived here and perhaps imbibed by policymakers. For one, it is not at all necessary to be an acknowledged scholar to be a successful leader in the world of academe. Yet, another insight that reveals itself here is that for true reforms and changes to take root, some long-term continuity in leadership is vital. Gwyer moved the university to its current campus, and his stamp can be seen and felt in much that makes this institution so celebrated. He transformed the undergraduate programmes in form and substance. They shifted from their two-year duration to a three-year length of study. This happened in the teeth of heavy opposition and a great deal of noise.

I, for one, can understand and sympathize with him and, thus, I also lay claim to some kinship. I say this without laying pretensions or claim to a similar stature. I see so many parallels and similarities between his efforts and what I had to face when I attempted to move the university to a four-year undergraduate programme from its three-year avatar. In any case, Gwyer succeeded in his efforts, and this set the tone for the rest of the nation. I, too, can lay claim—in all humility—to success, since the recently announced National Education Policy (NEP), 2020, is a near verbatim reproduction of what we put in place during my tenure at the university. Gwyer also introduced the honours programmes at the undergraduate level, and I had the good fortune to bring them up to speed by introducing much-needed flexibility in the form of multiple exit and entry points with academic credit banks, hands-on pedagogy and genuine transdisciplinary modes of learning blended with opportunities of entrepreneurship.

It was during Gwyer's time that a great flowering happened. The colleges began to come into their own. Great names and just as worthy traditions came to be associated with the colleges in various ways. Some of India's finest citizens began to pass through the portals of the colleges whose own numbers have swelled in tune with the needs of the nation. The colleges are, in many ways, the cornerstone and lifeblood of DU.

They define its character and attract extraordinary talent from all corners of the nation. They cater to the university's undergraduates. They enjoy a special status as constituent colleges of the university. This offers a far more meaningful compact between them and the university as opposed to the lowly status of merely being an affiliated college, as happens in most of India's universities.

This, too, marks the university as unique. Of course, this is borrowed—very much—from the Oxbridge model. I must also mention that the postgraduate and research programmes of the university have been of an extraordinary character as well. They are undertaken in the postgraduate departments, clustered in groups according to their streams of knowledge, which are formally called the faculties of the university. All this commenced from Gwyer's time. Gwyer was a true liberal and sympathetic to India's cause. This is borne out in many ways, but I personally am most fond of one particular episode.

During the 1942 Quit India movement, students of Ramjas College, Hindu College and St. Stephen's College indulged in violence on the campus. The viceroy wrote to Gwyer to take punitive action. Gwyer's actions do not betray any such reaction. On the other hand, he reportedly responded by asserting somewhat to the effect that they were youngsters giving vent to the aspirations of their country. There is no record of what the viceroy had to say after that.

Gwyer laid the structures of governance for the university, which were adopted subsequently as an Act of Parliament. It is a tribute to his wisdom that these regulations have stood the test of time. The Act that established the university is truly full of wisdom and depth. It envisages almost complete autonomy for the university and ensures that the vice chancellor is his own boss.

Gwyer also took full advantage of the displacement of several leading academics and scientists during the upheaval of Partition. He attracted them by offering positions with supporting perks at DU. This brought about a quantum change to the academic profile of the university. I am personally aware of so many individuals who joined the university and were famous, or who made a mark later in life. I once again see a sort of parallel with this in a limited but significant way. Just before I took charge as the vice chancellor, the university underwent a major and sudden expansion in student enrolment that also caused logistical upheavals. This increase in student numbers was caused by providing reserved seats to a large and underprivileged segment of society. Just as Partition brought talent to the university, so did the according of reservation for a whole new segment of India's underprivileged classes, thereby offering an enormous opportunity.

Today, a vast segment of our youth is being brought into our institutions of learning. These students have an eagerness and hunger that has added vigour to the university. The opportunity that this accords us is limitless. The four-year undergraduate programme (FYUP), which is essentially the NEP, has the potential to meet their needs and aspirations. In fact, in its avatar as the FYUP, we could well-nigh demonstrate the truth of this assertion. Let me hasten to add that the design of the NEP can help propel India into an altogether higher orbit as a nation.

The challenge that faces the university is that of streaming the needs and aspirations of the young minds of India in the right manner. I witnessed the huge returns that my efforts at reform brought for DU. We were consistently ranked—during the years 2011–15—as India's number one university, and our global rankings had begun to knock on the gates of the Top-200 club. I am glad to see that this trend has kicked on further, and DU's colleges are gaining even more ground in the more recent rankings. For the first time in the history of the university, innovation, invention and entrepreneurship became buzzwords at the undergraduate level. Start-ups from that time that have thrived together account for several million dollars' worth in terms of their recent valuations. These learnings and gains beckon India and are the surest and most natural way to take us into the realm of a knowledge economy. Undergraduates from during my time have begun to produce research and have started setting up start-ups.

We must also keep in mind the handicap that a vice chancellor at DU now faces in the form of a solitary five-year term. Gwyer was fortunate in that respect. Unfortunately, his journey at DU could have ended and needed to end in a better way. Alas, this seems to be the tradition of the vice chancellors at DU. Gwyer resigned abruptly in 1950 and left India. As the story goes, Sir Shri Ram, the then chairman of the Hindu College, apparently complained to the Visitor—none other than the president of India in his ex-officio capacity—about a perceived injustice that had been rendered to the Hindu College by Gwyer. As the story goes, Dr Rajendra Prasad spoke about this with Gwyer, who lost no time in putting in his papers. He moved back to England and died a couple of years later. Thus ended the saga of Maurice Gwyer at DU. There is no record whatsoever of his services ever having been formally recognized by India. Of course, Nehru was a frequent visitor during Gwyer's time—and even later—and the university awarded, in Gwyer's time, an honorary doctorate to him, Lord Mountbatten and to other luminaries.

Education and Agitation

My personal—albeit informal at the beginning—engagement with the university dates to 1969 when my father was invited to join the university as a professor of mathematics. He had already made a mark as a noticeably young mathematician at the Maharaja Sayajirao University of Baroda (Vadodara), and in recognition of his stature and work, he was invited to transform the rather lacklustre mathematics programme at Delhi. His formal association with DU happened almost in the middle of the Naxalite movement taking root at the university to some extent.

This was brought home to me one fine morning in 1970, when, as a schoolboy, I encountered bold front-page headlines in leading dailies of the day reporting to the world at large about an incident. It had so transpired that the rather conservative and staid St. Stephen's College was the centre of attention. Some of its students had scaled the formidable tower at St. Stephen's—undetected and in the middle of the night—to paint in bold red ink Maoist slogans calling for an armed revolution. Since then, my memories of DU are peppered to a significant extent with various agitations. Of course, this does not imply that DU was not making strides in the realm of scholarship and education.

Allow me a moment to remember these agitations—which have continued to occur time and again—since they highlight a special feature of the university at several points of its journey, particularly in the past 50 years. In 1972, I enrolled as a freshman at St. Stephen's in the BA (Honours) in Mathematics programme. It had been drilled into me and into the other 'freshers' that St. Stephen's was a nursery for the civil services and the aim of many of its students was simply to get into India's elite civil services. It, thus, came as a highly unexpected but not unwelcome surprise to me when I learnt that, for the first time in the more than 90-year history of St. Stephen's, students had gone on strike and had walked out of their classrooms. The trigger for the agitation was something as mundane as the raising of the mess food charges for students who were residing in the halls of residence of the college. This raising of the mess charges had affected only a third of the student body, but there was near unanimity on the part of the entire student body of the college to go on strike.

For me, the best part was that I had a whole week off from college classes. Sadly, the college gave in after a week and order was restored. On a lighter note, I gained a very valuable insight that has stood me in good stead in my later years as an academic administrator—any move to mess around with food prices has to be handled with great care and sensitivity! Throughout my journey with the university, I have witnessed so many such events and upheavals that I shall have to put them in a separate essay. I must also state that several teachers' movements and even some student agitations that originated from the university have impacted the nation's journey in their own ways.

Spearheading India's Growth Story

I could recount, in endless fashion, the grand achievements that have been associated with the university in so many realms of human endeavour. Several of them I have witnessed first-hand, such as the effects of the Bangladesh war, the dark days of the Emergency, the Mandal agitation, and the impact of the age of computers and the attendant IT revolution. I could also recount the great names that the university has been associated with from the very same pages of its history. I have seen the many triumphs and several vicissitudes in the journey of my alma mater. It has endured them all and has served our nation well. I leave these tales to be told another time and in other ways or perhaps by better storytellers. What I do wish to state here with vigour and clarity is that DU enjoys a very special stature, and commands attention and respect across India and even abroad.

In many ways, I see no distinction between India and DU. They reside in each other. The university is uniquely poised at this juncture in time and history, when it has completed a hundred years, to lead the way for India's journey into the future. I repeat once again with all the earnestness at my command that India and DU must seize this opportunity. Then and only then will the university prove wrong the predictions of men such as the Harvard intellectual Joseph Nye that India will not dominate the twenty-first century simply because its universities are not good enough. If DU builds on its experiences, and learnings of its ideas and experiments of the recent past that have led to the creation of the NEP, it may well—and it must—then spearhead India's growth story.

JOURNEY OF A HUNDRED YEARS

Sanjeev Sanyal

The Delhi University was established in 1922.[1] It was originally envisaged as a unitary teaching and residential university by the Delhi University Act, 1922, passed by the then central Legislative Assembly. The capital of British India had been shifted to the city barely 11 years earlier, and the new capital was still being built. What we now know as Old Delhi was the main urban cluster, and the Civil Lines area to the north was the main administrative hub.

At the time, there were already four colleges in Delhi: St. Stephen's College, founded in 1881; Hindu College, founded in 1899; Ramjas College, founded in 1917; and Lady Hardinge Medical College for Women started in 1916.[2]

---

[1]Annual Report of Delhi University, 1922–23.

[2]A fifth college, much older in existence, was also present in Delhi at the time. Today's Zakir Husain Delhi College (renamed in honour of Dr Zakir Husain in 1975—and others—who revived the Delhi College as a non-denominational institution in 1948) finds its antecedents in colleges dating back to 1696 and can lay claim to being the oldest existing educational institution in India. As the Anglo-Arabic Intermediate College,

The first four colleges were affiliated to Punjab University before the establishment of the new university in Delhi. DU started with three out of these four colleges, i.e. St. Stephens, Ramjas and Hindu (Lady Hardinge College continued to be affiliated to Punjab University and became affiliated with DU as its Faculty of Medical Sciences in 1950). Two faculties, i.e. Arts and Science, were established, and 750 students[3] signed up in the first year. The Faculty of Law was established in 1924 as a result of a petition submitted by a group of leading citizens in the previous year.

The original intention of the Act—of a unitary structure—was soon abandoned in light of the demand from the colleges that their separate identities be preserved. Thus, the university as it developed was neither unitary nor entirely residential (although many colleges would later have hostels). It functioned largely as a collection of associated colleges, loosely federated together. It had no building of its own, and its administrative offices were housed in rented accommodation successively on Under Hill Road, Alipur Road and the Old Secretariat. It was shifted to its present site in 1933.[4]

When the university was allotted its site, it comprised only a few government bungalows, possibly built for the viceroy's staff, horse stables, and quarters for bandmasters and servants.[5]

it was affiliated to DU in 1925.

[3]Basu, Aparna (ed.), *University of Delhi, 1922–1997: Platinum Jubilee*, University of Delhi, 1998.

[4]Ibid.

[5]This information was provided by Prof. Saini, the librarian of DU.

However, this site could not be handed over immediately, as the revolutionaries Bhagat Singh and Batukeshwar Dutt were being housed there as they awaited their court trial (it is commonly believed that Bhagat Singh was kept in a dark, dingy basement underneath the present-day Academic Council Hall).

The site allotted to the university had considerable historical significance as it was next to the 'Ridge'. Many Stone Age tools and other artefacts have been found in the area.[6] Among these artefacts, an Ashoka pillar was also found. The Ridge had also been the main British position during the Revolt of 1857–58, from where they had bombarded the walled city of Shahjahanabad. And the British had built a Mutiny Memorial there in 1863 to commemorate the officers and men who had died during the siege of Delhi.

An Era of Awakening

The university started as a local institution catering primarily to Delhi students but made steady progress in the first 25 years. One by one, new institutions were added with strong support from the business community in particular. Some of these institutions existed even before DU was established. The Commercial High School, for instance, was set up by the Commercial Education Trust at Charkhewalan

---

[6]This information appeared in an article by Dr Surajit Sinha in *Man and India*, and was provided to Ms Aparna Basu by Dr Nanyanjyot Lahiri, Reader in the Department of History, DU.

in the walled city in 1920. The trust itself was established a few months earlier on the day of Basant Panchami by seven leading businessmen, headed by renowned industrialist Lala Shri Ram. The school introduced a Post-Matriculation Diploma Programme in Commerce under the supervision of R.K. Kumar, who later became the first principal of Commercial College. The inauguration of Commercial College initiated commerce education in Delhi. The first batch of students was enrolled on the first floor of a 'hall' opposite the St. James' Church at Kashmere Gate. The classes began with 12 students and four faculty members from a hired bungalow at 8, Darya Ganj, New Delhi.

In 1926, Commercial College got affiliated to DU; we know it today as Shri Ram College of Commerce or more colloquially as SRCC. Six years later, it was upgraded to the status of a degree college and started awarding its graduates the BA (Pass) Commerce degree of the university. The college launched its annual magazine *Yamuna* in January 1928. The BA (Honours) in Commerce was introduced in 1943; it was renamed BCom a few years later. The same year witnessed the introduction of the MA (Economics) course, followed by the introduction of the MA (Commerce) in 1948.

In 1924, the newly established DU gave recognition to the Indraprastha Girls' Intermediate College, the roots of which can be traced to the push for widening higher education to women given by some of the leading members of Delhi's business community in the early twentieth century. A small primary school called Indraprastha Putri Pathshala was opened in 1904 for girls in Chippiwara Street, overlooking the Jama Masjid, in what is now Old Delhi. Lala Jugal Kishore went from house to house in the predominantly Hindu locality to get families to send their daughters to the school. Rai Bahadur Balkrishna Das donated a large haveli with two courtyards for the school in 1906.

By the 1920s, many of the students of this school wanted to pursue higher studies. A small 'college' was started for them on the roof of the school, but it soon became clear that this would be inadequate. Larger premises were now needed, and a request was sent to the government. Alipore House, the former office-cum-residence of the commander-in-chief of the British Indian Army, had recently been vacated when officials moved to New Delhi. After a few years of protracted negotiations, Alipore House was leased to the Indraprastha (IP) College for Women in 1937. IP College still functions from the same location. Many of the old colonial-era buildings in the college premises have been preserved and are in active use.[7]

Tryst with the Freedom Struggle

Delhi's college students have always engaged with the social, political and economic changes around them. Even before the university was founded, students and faculty of St. Stephen's and Hindu were active during the Swadeshi movement of 1905–06. After the execution of Khudiram Bose and Prafulla Chaki, the

[7]Kamath, Shanti and Narain Prasad, *The Saga of Indraparastha College for Women*, Indraprastha Educational Trust, 1999.

reading rooms of these colleges became centres of revolutionary talk and political discussions. *Yugantar* leaflets were widely circulated among college students.[8] Several students would join an underground network built by revolutionary leader Rash Behari Bose, who carried out a major attack on Viceroy Lord Hardinge in Chandni Chowk in 1912.

Lala Har Dayal was an exceptionally talented student of St. Stephen's, where he briefly taught as well. He left India in 1908 to study at Oxford, where he came under the influence of Vinayak Damodar Savarkar, who had created a revolutionary network in Europe. After Savarkar's arrest, he escaped to the United States, where he founded the Ghadar movement.[9] The Ghadarites in North America, in coordination with Rash Behari's revolutionary network in India, would attempt to cause a large-scale revolt in the Indian Army during the First World War. The attempt would fail, but would inspire the formation of the Indian National Army (INA) during the Second World War.

After the First World War, the non-cooperation movement attracted several students and teachers. In November 1920, Mahatma Gandhi formally opened the National School in Delhi, which was founded by famous lawyer and freedom fighter Asaf Ali. He also paid a visit to St. Stephen's, where he addressed a joint meeting of the students of St. Stephen's, Hindu and Ramjas. A.T. Gidwani, the principal of Ramjas

---

[8]Borkar, Suhas, 'At the Altar of National Freedom', *The Stephanian* 1972–73, pp. 1–5.
[9]Ibid. 6–11.

College, resigned and openly supported the non-cooperation movement. There was active participation of the university in the civil disobedience movement in 1930, including a complete strike and boycott of foreign clothes. The national flag was unfurled both in Ramjas and St. Stephen's.[10] As can be imagined, the colonial authorities were not pleased by these developments.

During the Quit India movement in August 1942, a vociferous gathering of students from Hindu and IP College collected outside the gates of St. Stephen's and urged Stephanians to join them in a procession in support of the Congress leaders who had been jailed the previous day. About half of the college made its way out through the back gate and across the university grounds to join demonstrators. For several days, the atmosphere was charged with tension, classes were not held and there was police action against the protesting students.

Similarly, during the INA trials in 1946, Sameeruddin Khan, a Stephanian, was successful in disrupting the morning assembly, and with 50 to 100 boys who boycotted classes, went on a protest march. He pulled down the Union Jack from the flagstaff.[11] With the Royal Indian Navy in open revolt in Bombay (now Mumbai), the British finally decided to end their occupation of the country.

---

[10]Vatts, Meenalochana, 'Politics and Society in Delhi, 1920–1934', PhD Thesis, Kurukshetra University, 1983, pp. 127–28.

[11]Bhattacharya, Aditya, 'From an Ivory Tower', *The Stephanian*, vol. 88, no. 1, 1978–79, pp. 19–20.

Of course, not all students joined the freedom movement or served the national cause. Mohammad Zia-ul-Haq, a graduate in history from St. Stephen's in 1943, would join the army and fight for the British cause during the Second World War in Myanmar and Indonesia, and later shift to the Pakistan Army after Partition, and would rise to become the country's army chief in 1976. A year later, he would seize power in a military coup and crown himself president.[12]

Becoming a Field of Ambition

Despite the disruptions caused by the freedom struggle, the university continued to expand. Under the leadership of Sir Maurice Gwyer, who was appointed vice chancellor in 1938, the university grew in leaps and bounds. He prepared a vision to improve the institution.[13] The main features of his vision were the establishment of a number of professorial chairs and readerships; scholarships and other facilities for postgraduate study and research for young men of talent; a better library and sports facilities; and, most importantly, a three-year degree course. The Government of India introduced a Bill in the Legislative Assembly to amend the

---

[12]Krishnan, Revathi, 'Zia-ul-Haq, the Stephanian Pakistani dictator who feared Indira Gandhi', *ThePrint,* 17 August 2019, https://tinyurl.com/m5auj2s8. Accessed on 18 May 2022.

[13]Basu, Aparna, 'Foundation and Early History of Delhi University', *Delhi Through the Ages: Essays in Urban History, Culture and Society*, R.E. Frykenberg (ed.), Oxford University Press, New Delhi, 1986.

Delhi University Act to provide three-year BA and BSc pass and honours degree courses. Nonetheless, at the time of Independence, there were only six degree colleges in the university, and only three faculties: Arts, Science and Law.

With Partition, millions of refugees poured into Delhi from West Punjab and the North-West Frontier Province (NWFP). As a result, Delhi's population increased from 488,452 in 1921 to 1,744,072 in 1951.[14] Between 1941 and 1951, the population almost doubled.[15] This was bound to have repercussions on the university. When the displaced students sought admission, the university had to adopt new regulations and relax existing ones. The last date of admission was extended, a special admission examination was held, and Hindu, Ramjas and IP colleges were permitted to run second-shift classes, teaching courses based on the Punjab University syllabus.

New colleges were started as well. Among the colleges started in the 1950s were Sri Guru Tegh Bahadur (SGTB) Khalsa College, Janki Devi Memorial College, Pannalal Girdharlal Dayanand Anglo-Vedic (PGDAV) College, Sanatan Dharma College (rechristened Atma Ram Sanatan Dharma College in 1968) and Deshbandhu College. With new colleges being set up in different parts of an ever-expanding city, the Delhi University Act was amended again in 1952, making it a teaching and affiliating university. The university was to have

---

[14]Thapliyal, Uma Prasad, *Gazetteer of Rural Delhi,* Gazetteer Unit, Delhi Administration, 1987, p. 32.

[15]Ibid.

constituent colleges, i.e. those who offered honours courses, and affiliating colleges that enrolled students for the pass degree.

Economist and institution builder Dr V.K.R.V. Rao envisaged setting up a world-class department of economics. At his initiative, the Delhi School of Economics (DSE) was set up in 1949.[16] The DSE housed not only the department of economics but also those of commerce, management, sociology, human geography and an agro-economic research centre. The Institute of Economic Growth (IEG) was founded in 1958 by him. Both DSE and IEG have gone on to become institutions of great repute. Their campuses are right next to each other in the heart of the university.

In the 1960s, the university again started experiencing an unprecedented pressure for enrolment as more and more students from across India began to come to Delhi to study. The number of students in the university increased from 4,166 in 1947–48 to 7,149 in 1951–52, 21,918 in 1961–62 and 96,515 in 1971–72. To ease this pressure of growing numbers, new colleges were established, such as Daulat Ram College, Lakshmibai College, Kamala Nehru College, Gargi College and Maitreyi College. Around 95 per cent funding of the colleges came from the University Grants Commission (UGC), and it was not in a position to fund more colleges. Hence, many of these new colleges were established and funded by the Delhi administration. The School of Correspondence Courses was

---

[16] Dhar, P.N., 'The Early Years', *Reflections on the Delhi School of Economics*, Dharma Kumar and Dilip Mokerjee (eds), Oxford University Press, Delhi, 1995.

started in 1962—the first in the country to start such a course.

With a view to limit the growing size of postgraduate classes on the main campus, easing transport problems for South Delhi students and as part of the university's phased programme of decentralization, a postgraduate centre was established in July 1970 in Sri Venkateswara College near Dhaula Kuan. Classes for Hindi, English and commerce were started, and thanks to the initiative taken by the then vice chancellor, Dr Sarup Singh, South Campus was started in 1973.

Beyond Scholarly Success

With students from across India, DU has become a bellwether for national political, social and economic trends. Winning the Delhi University Students Union (DUSU) elections, or even individual college elections, can be used as a stepping stone for aspiring politicians to directly enter local or national politics. There are many leaders who were once a part of DUSU and later occupied important positions in the government, such as Arun Jaitley, Vijay Goel and Ajay Maken.

Till 1972, student elections were indirect. The colleges would first elect 10 councillors, who would then elect the DUSU president and vice president. Arun Jaitley, who was the president of the students' union at SRCC at that time, led a prolonged students' agitation (from November 1972 to January 1973) along with fellow Akhil Bharatiya Vidyarthi Parishad (ABVP) members in support of these reforms. Tens of thousands of students joined the strike for over 50 days.

This strike resulted in the university administration changing the DUSU election system from indirect to direct mode.

After he joined the Faculty of Law, Jaitley was elected the DUSU president as an ABVP candidate, in 1974, a year before the Emergency. He would play a visible role in pushing back against Prime Minister Indira Gandhi's Emergency rule. In a blog titled 'Remembering Emergency', Jaitley reminisced:

> At about 2 AM past midnight, I received a knock at my residence. The police had come to arrest me. My father, a lawyer by profession got into an argument outside the gate of my house asking them at least to inform him as to the nature of offence I had committed. The police had simple instructions to arrest me – they did not know under which provision and for which offence. While this argument was on, I escaped from the backdoor and went to the friend's house in the neighbourhood.[17]

The government had blacked out information and gagged the media, but information trickled in that senior opposition leaders had been arrested. Jaitley made his way under cover to the university campus.

> Along with my co-ABVP workers, I reached Delhi University Campus by about 10.00am to organise a protest. This was the only protest against the Emergency

[17]'Remembering Emergency', Arun Jaitley, 25 June 2014, https://tinyurl.com/5n8wjta5. Accessed on 18 May 2022.

> which took place that day in the whole country. An effigy was burned by us in protest. The news of the protest attracted a large number of policemen in the Delhi University campus. I requested my colleagues to quietly disappear since I had been surrounded by the police. I courted arrest. I was also taken to the Timarpur Police Station where I was handed over a detention order under the Maintenance of Internal Security Act (MISA). I was taken to the Tihar jail in Delhi where other political detainees were also kept.[18]

Jaitley was released after two years, on 25 January 1977. Two days later, the ABVP took Jaitley in a large procession to every college of the university campus, which saw massive student participation. Thus, DU had again been at the forefront of a major political event in India's history.

The students would again rise in protest in August 1990 when Prime Minister V.P. Singh announced the implementation of the Mandal Commission Report, reserving 27 per cent seats for the Other Backward Castes (OBCs). There were protests across India, but DU would be at the forefront. Rajeev Goswami from Deshbandhu College was the first person to publicly immolate himself in protest, sustaining 50 per cent burns. He was saved and went on to become the president of DUSU a year later. However, he never quite recovered fully and succumbed to jaundice in 2004, at the age of 33. The self-immolation by Goswami started a series of attempted suicides.

---

[18]Ibid.

In cities and towns near Delhi, a number of youths set themselves on fire. Students boycotted classes, protested at Kingsway camp and sat on dharnas at the crossing outside Ramjas. V.P. Singh's attempts to further politicize the issue only resulted in deepening social divisions. A rally at the Boat Club, called by farmers from Haryana in support of the students' movement, attracted large crowds to the centre of Delhi. The rally got violent, and three people died in police firing. Although these protests were eventually put down, it triggered a sequence of events that caused the fall of the government and a sharp decline in V.P. Singh's political fortunes.

The Changing Aesthetic

Despite the angst of the anti-Mandal agitation, the mood on the campus took a more optimistic turn from the 1990s. After the economic crisis of 1990–91, the economy was systematically liberalized. The focus of students steadily shifted away from agitational politics and preparations for civil services examinations to looking for private-sector jobs. By the early 2000s, major private-sector corporates and even foreign companies began to visit the campus to recruit graduates. The flow of talent visibly turned towards management schools and the open job market. This trend gathered even more pace between 2010 and 2020, as an increasing proportion of students began to aspire to become innovators and entrepreneurs. Finance and management courses became increasingly popular, and new courses were introduced. Those who would have once aspired to the civil services are today more likely to opt for start-ups. The founding fathers of many colleges, drawn from Delhi's business community, would have been pleased.

Growing economic prosperity, corporate sponsorships and support from successful alumni have also changed the aesthetic of the campus in recent years. Buildings and grounds are usually better maintained these days; the canteens, cleaner. College festivals are elaborate events with significant prize money compared to the relatively amateur affairs earlier. Wealthier colleges like SRCC have fully air-conditioned facilities; IP College has an impressive museum; Hindu College, a fascinating science block. The packed University Special buses have mostly been replaced by the relative efficiency of the Metro railways system. Many students now own cars or motorbikes—a rarity till the 1990s. Mobile phones mean that linkages across colleges are now more likely. The cafes in today's Kamla Nagar market are a long way from the hole-in-the-wall chai shops of the past. The students in South Campus have even more choices. This does not mean that there are no problems. Issues ranging from faculty recruitment to syllabus upgradation remain thorny. Meanwhile, the university continues to provide succour and act as a venue for major political movements in India even today.

Connecting with 'Mouse Charmers'

In 2013, Narendra Modi, the then chief minister of Gujarat, delivered the annual Shri Ram Memorial Oration lecture at

SRCC's indoor sports stadium amid nearly 2,000 students. The theme of his 75-minute talk was 'Emerging Business Models in the Global Scenario'. In an inspiring speech, Modi discussed youth, development and governance. These remained the keywords of his speech, hard-selling the Gujarat model of development. 'India must learn from global examples to become a global leader. The 21st century belongs to us. We just need to rebrand our country.'[19] Pitching for the importance of good governance, Modi said, 'We need P2G2. Pro-People Good Governance' as the guiding principle.[20]

The main reason why his speech struck a chord with the young audience—he received a standing ovation—was that his positive message was a change from the usual angry rhetoric of an earlier generation of politicians and was more in tune with the prevailing mood. He spoke of the youth as a 'new-age power and not just new-age voters ... 65 per cent of the population below 35 years of age. Europe has grown old, China is old, but India is young. Unfortunately, we have not been able to harness such a big demographic opportunity.' He termed the country's youth as 'mouse-charmers'—a reference to the computer mouse: 'We are no longer a country of snake-charmers, we have become a country of mouse-charmers. Our

---

[19]Menon, Aditya, 'Modi charms students of DU college with Gujarat story, says this century belongs to India', *India Today*, 6 February 2013, https://bit.ly/3LKJG1I. Accessed on 4 May 2022.

[20]'10 punch lines from Narendra Modi's speech at SRCC', *The Economic Times*, 6 February 2013, https://tinyurl.com/4d8r5ycf. Accessed on 9 May 2022.

youth are ruling the world with their mastery of the mouse.'[21] The speech launched a campaign that led directly to a historic election victory.

An Institution of Eminence

Beginning with three colleges and 750 students, DU has grown to become one of the largest and most prestigious universities in India with 16 faculties, over 80 academic departments, an equal number of colleges and over seven lakh students.[22] The university was granted the status of Institution of Eminence (IoE) by the Government of India in 2019.[23]

However, as it completes a century of existence, we must recognize that the institution faced some of its most difficult times in 2020 and 2021 due to the Covid-19 pandemic. As the world reeled from the virus, the university was effectively closed to students for almost two years. Traditional classrooms, where teaching and learning was transacted, were completely replaced by online platforms. All this needed innovation that would have been unimaginable a few years earlier. Students were able to write their examinations from their homes, and

---

[21]Menon, Aditya, 'Modi charms students of DU college with Gujarat story, says this century belongs to India', *India Today*, 6 February 2013, https://bit.ly/3LKJG1I. Accessed on 4 May 2022.

[22]University of Delhi, https://tinyurl.com/muar58pm. Accessed on 18 May 2022.

[23]'20 Institution recommended for status of "Institutions of Eminence"', Press Information Bureau, Government of India, 2 August 2019, https://tinyurl.com/482urd78. Accessed on 18 May 2022.

teachers were able to evaluate through electronic means. To expand its landscape of e-learning and teaching, the university launched the One-DU portal. It has enhanced accessibility to learning, fostered best practices and promoted professional development by harnessing the benefits of available educational technologies.

For all the application of technology, the college experience cannot be replaced by a Zoom call. There is a joy in chatting with classmates on the lawns or taking part in an inter-college event. As I write these words in mid-February 2022, the colleges are finally opening up again, and students and teachers are enthusiastically trooping back to their campuses. DU looks forward to another century.

The author would like to thank Dr Aasheerwad Dwivedi and Ms Mahima for their research support in preparing this essay.

REMEMBERING DU VIA STEPHANIA

Shashi Tharoor

Some years ago, I received a gushing fan letter from someone who had chanced upon a copy of the programme brochure of the St. Stephen's College Shakespeare Society production of *Antony and Cleopatra* in 1974. She couldn't believe her eyes at the galaxy of names on the cast list. The title roles were played by me and a young Mira Nair (St. Stephen's, all-male in those days, borrowed its female thespians from Miranda House and repaid the compliment in kind—the previous year, I had taken the lead in Miranda's production of Bertolt Brecht's *St. Joan of the Stockyards*). Pompey was Aamir Raza Husain, who would go on to become a renowned theatre director and impresario; Enobarbus, Ramu Damodaran, later private secretary to Prime Minister P.V. Narasimha Rao; Roman legionaries included Arun Singh, Asoke Mukerji and Gautam Mukhopadhaya, our former ambassadors to the United States (US), United Nations (UN) and Myanmar, respectively; and amongst the slaves and spear-carriers stood the brilliant novelist-to-be Amitav Ghosh and the future advertising guru Piyush Pandey. 'All of you together on one stage!' gushed the fan. 'What was it like? Did you all have a sense of destiny, knowing what you would become?'

I no longer recall my reply, but I don't believe any of us were unduly concerned about what we would become: at college, we just were. Delhi University in my time (1972–75) was that kind of place. And if the fan had known about the Stephanian 'ShakeSoc types', who for one reason or the other didn't act in that particular production, she would have had even more to be awestruck about. The likes of Kabir Bedi and Roshan Seth, Stephanian stage legends both (as, in a slightly more modest vein, was Kapil Sibal), had passed out a couple of years ago. But Rajiv Mehrotra, already a TV star on Doordarshan, declined to audition, while future novelists Rukun Advani and Anurag Mathur didn't make the cut, and celebrity-quizmaster-to-be Siddhartha Basu, much to everyone's surprise, auditioned but was passed over for a role (he instead wrote an acerbic review of the production in the campus newspaper *Kooler Talk* [known to Stephanians as 'KT' or 'Katie'], describing my Antony as a 'flippant, underfed Romeo').

Sense of destiny? Not consciously, except in the sense that by getting into college, you had already arrived; there was an implicit sense that the possibilities were limitless. Yet, none of us would have felt that there was anything particularly unusual about our peers. St. Stephen's, in those days, simply attracted people like that.

Hindsight, however, prompts something of the sense of wonderment apparent in the anonymous Wikipedia entry that informs the world, rather breathlessly, that my 'contemporaries included the politician Salman Khurshid, the documentary filmmaker Rajiv Mehrotra, the quizmaster Siddhartha Basu, the novelists Amitav Ghosh, Rukun Advani and Anurag Mathur, the theatre impresario Aamir Raza Husain, the editor and politician Chandan Mitra, the columnist Swapan Dasgupta, the economist and media crusader Paranjoy Guha Thakurta, the IAS officer-turned social activist Harsh Mander, the television personality Sunil Sethi, the diplomats Jayant Prasad, the World Trade Organization (WTO) executive Harsha Vardhana Singh and the advertising guru Piyush Pandey.' It's true, they did—plus test cricketer Arun Lal, the composer Param Vir and a slew of IAS officers (I recently counted 17 secretaries to the Government of India whom I had known at St. Stephen's) were guys we hung out with at the dhaba, borrowed tutorial notes from, complained about the mess food to, cut classes and saw movies, and competed for female attention with—not A-listers of the future of whom we should have been in awe.

In those days, I thought of Amitav Ghosh as a bright and rather persistent campus reporter for All India Radio's 'roving microphone'. Piyush Pandey might, I hoped, play cricket for India one day, as his rustic manner and Hindi colloquialisms seemed to have nothing to do with the country's prevailing advertising culture. After voting for Salman Khurshid and seeing him trounced in the election for the college presidency, I did not imagine the glittering political future that awaited him on the national stage. Harsh Mander's passionate engagement in social service work, though, already prefigured the idealist

IAS officer and NGO activist he would soon become. When I borrowed 'tutes' from an intense and soft-spoken Param Vir, I had no idea he would one day be hailed as a genius composer on London's West End. And today's IAS heavyweights include Stephanians who were inveterate punsters, practical jokers and participants in the drag contest to elect a 'Miss Fresher'—hardly material, at first sight, to be finance secretary one day.

And yet, what does the very name 'St. Stephen's' convey to outsiders? Let's face it: to non-Stephanians, the term 'St. Stephen's' conjures up three overlapping concepts, none of which are meant to be flattering: elitism, Anglophilia and deracination (there is even a rather obscure dictionary definition of a Stephanian as a 'charcoal fossil'—a kind of rock, of course, but charcoal fossil's metaphorical possibilities are enough to start a chortle amongst many of the college's self-deprecating alumni).

A Spirit Called Stephanian

When I was given the rare privilege of delivering the 125th Anniversary Golden Jubilee Lecture at the college in 2005 (the 100th anniversary had featured another old boy, Pakistan's then president, Muhammad Zia-ul-Haq), I was able to take for granted that few in the audience (which included serving and former Cabinet Ministers, ambassadors and generals, not to mention the assortment of CEOs and cricket stars) would contest that there is a spirit that can be called Stephania (most of us had spent three or five years living in and celebrating it).

Stephania was both an ethos and a condition to which we aspired. Elitism—elitism of merit, not birth—was part of it, but by no means the whole.

In any case, 'Mission College' elitism was still elitism in an Indian context, albeit one shaped, like so many Indian institutions, by a colonial legacy. There is no denying that the aim of the Cambridge Brotherhood in founding St. Stephen's in 1881 was to produce more obedient subjects to serve Her Britannic Majesty; their idea of constructive missionary activity was to bring the intellectual and social atmosphere of Camside to the dry, dust plains of Delhi. Improbably enough, they succeeded, and the resultant hybrid outlasted the Raj.

The St. Stephen's I knew in the early 1970s was an institution whose students sustained a Shakespeare Society and a Criterion Club, and organized 'Union Debates' on such subjects as 'In the opinion of this House, the opinion of this House does not matter'. We staged plays and wrote poetry, and the Wodehouse Society I revived ran India's only faculty-sanctioned 'Practical Joke Competition' (in memory of P.G. Wodehouse's irrepressible Lord Ickenham). It was St. Stephen's that invented the 'Winter Festival' of collegiate cultural competition, which was imitated at universities across the country. If that sounds deplorably effete, we invariably reached the annual inter-college cricket final and turned up in large numbers to cheer the Stephanian cricketers on to their accustomed victory (one of my few worthwhile innovations as president of the students' union, aside from improving the mess food on 'vegetarian day', was to supply throat lozenges free of charge to the more raucous of our cheerleaders at the cricket final. I am told this is one more Stephanian tradition that, along with our cricket team, has bitten the dust).

We maintained a careful distinction between the 'Junior Common Room' and the 'Senior Combination Room', and allowed the world's only non-Cantabridgian 'gyps' to serve our meals and make our beds. And if the punts never came to the Jamuna, the puns flowed on the pages of *Kooler Talk* and the cyclostyled Wodehouse Society rag *Spice* (whose typing mistakes, in Ramu Damodaran's hands, were deliberate and deliberately hilarious).

This was the St. Stephen's I knew, and none of us who lived and breathed the Stephanian air saw any alien affectation in it. For one thing, St. Stephen's also embraced the Hindi movies at Kamla Nagar, the trips to Sukhiya's dhaba and the *chowchow* at TibMon (as the Tibetan monastery was called by Stephanians); the nocturnal 'Informal Discussion Group' saw articulate discussions on political issues, and the 'Social Service League' actually went out and performed social service; and even for the 'pseuds', the height of career aspiration was the IAS, not some firang multinational. The Stephanian could hardly be deracinated and still manage to bloom. It was against Indian targets that the Stephanian set his goals, and by Indian assumptions that he sought to attain them (feminists, please do not object to my pronouns: I only knew St. Stephen's before its co-edification).

At the same time, St. Stephen's was, astonishingly for a college in Delhi, insulated to a remarkable extent from the prejudices of middle-class Indian life. It mattered little where you were from, which Indian language you spoke at home, what version of religious faith you espoused. When I joined college in 1972 from Calcutta, the son of a Keralite newspaper executive, I did not have to worry about fitting in—we were all minorities at St. Stephen's, and all part of one eclectic polychrome culture. Five of the preceding 10 union presidents had been non-Delhiite, non-Hindus (four Muslims and a Christian), and they had all been fairly elected against candidates from the 'majority' community. But at St. Stephen's, religion and region were not the distinctions that mattered; what counted was whether you were 'in residence' or a 'dayski' (day scholar), a 'science type' or a 'ShakeSoc type', a sportsman or a univ topper (or, best of all, both). Caste and creed were no bar, but these other categories determined your share of the Stephanian experience.

This blurring of conventional distinctions was a crucial element of Stephania. 'Sparring' with the more congenial of your comrades in residence—though it could leave you with a near-fatal faith in coffee, conversation and crosswords as ends in themselves—was manifestly more important than attending classes. And, in any case, you learned as much from approachable faculty members—like David Baker, Mohammad Amin (affectionately called Amin Sahib), Ranjit Bhatia, P.S. Dwivedi, Vinod Chowdhury and others too numerous to mention—outside the classroom as inside it. It was at one of Amin Sahib's mediaeval history lectures that he memorably translated the words inscribed above the stage in the college hall: Jesus said, 'I am the Light of the World' as '*Jesus ne kaha, main Noor Jehan hoon*'.

Being ragged outside the back gate of Miranda House, having a late coffee in your block tutor's room, hearing outrageous (and largely apocryphal) tales about recent Stephanians who were no longer around to contradict them, seeing your name punned with in KT, were all integral parts of the Stephanian culture, and of the ways in which this culture was transmitted to each successive batch of Stephanians. Debating with the more illustrious students of other DU colleges was like a rite of initiation: my very first debate, as a freshman, put me up against the formidable Hardeep Singh Puri of Hindu College, a famous name then already, studying for his master's. I managed to win and am grateful that this did not prevent him from becoming a friend in later life—as an illustrious member of the Indian Foreign Service (IFS) and, subsequently, as a minister in Prime Minister Narendra Modi's government—and he was remarkably helpful, during the first Covid-19 lockdown, in repatriating hundreds of my constituents stranded abroad.

My engagement with the broader university was limited: debates, of course, especially at Hindu College, were a major element of our life within DU. Our visits to the bank, the Coffee House and (mercifully rarely) the administrative offices, largely circumscribed our areas of involvement with broader university life. We participated, of course, in some pan-university events. I was made to feel extravagantly proud for winning the Rector's Prize in 1973 for the 'Best

Undergraduate Student' at DU, a distinction based on little more than the ability to keep one's head during a combative interview. My interest in the teachings of Swami Vivekananda also led to my being asked to deliver DU's annual Vivekananda Memorial Oration lecture in my final year there, the first-ever undergraduate to do so.

Political Avatars

Like other Stephanians, I did, however, have an ambiguous relationship with the hothouse world of Indian politics outside the campus. Our students' union, of which I won the presidency with 65 per cent of the vote in a three-cornered contest in 1974, was explicitly apolitical. The party-affiliated bodies that dominated DU campus politics at the time—the Jana Sangh's Akhil Bharatiya Vidyarthi Parishad (ABVP), starring a certain Arun Jaitley of Shri Ram College of Commerce (SRCC); the Congress-backed National Students' Union of India (NSUI); and the communist Students' Federation of India (SFI) and All India Students' Federation (AISF)—were not allowed to set up branches at St. Stephen's, and we were not members of Jaitley's Delhi University Students Union (DUSU). Our union was even called a 'society' till I persuaded the principal to allow us to call ourselves a 'Students' Union Society'.

Yet, some of us were to go on to develop political avatars. My campaign manager in 1974 and chancellor of the exchequer in my cabinet was Chandan Mitra, in those days a passionate leftist (as was his then-Trotskyite pal Swapan

Dasgupta). Both went on to become avatars of the political right that has now come into ascendancy in New Delhi. I myself did not conceal my sympathies for the Swatantra Party and my bitter disappointment at its dissolution and merger into Charan Singh's Bharatiya Lok Dal (BLD) in 1974, which I expressed publicly in the college auditorium when Piloo Mody addressed the student body that year. It is to St. Stephen's that I can trace the roots of my current dismay at the dwindling space for liberal ideas in our political discourse and my determination, from within the Congress party, to stand up for the values of democratic freedom, personal liberty, social liberalism, pluralism and individual initiative that Rajaji (C. Rajagopalachari), (Minoo) Masani and Mody had so brilliantly articulated in my youth (indeed, I find it ironic that some notably illiberal voices should have cornered the market on 'liberal' thought in our country).

I had graduated and left for studies in the US when the Emergency came, allowing the college authorities to suspend elections and appoint a student president—none other than my deputy Chandan Mitra! Many DU students opposed the Emergency with courage; some were even arrested, and some went 'underground' to evade arrest. Stephanians were widely assumed to have stayed aloof from it all, in keeping with their apolitical ethos. But contemporaries who stayed on at St. Stephen's have told me of subtler and more typically Stephanian resistance to the dictates of the Emergency. The Sanjay Gandhi slogan 'More Work Less Talk' quickly became transmuted, at St. Stephen's, to 'More Workless Talk'. Its Hindi version, '*Baatein Kam, Kaam Zyadah*', received a pointed rejoinder in a notice pinned on a board in the college's senior staff room: '*Baatein Kam, Chai Zyadah* (Less Talk, More Tea)'.

One incident from my final year remains vividly in my memory. A distinguished Stephanian addressed the college's annual Games Dinner of 1974–75, which I, never proficient at games of any sort, was invited to attend as the elected president of the union. He was an IFS officer with remarkable connections—married to royalty, a friend and confidante of the Nehru–Gandhi family, an author and diplomat of distinction. Yet, he surveyed us, 17- to 22-year-olds with bright eyes and scrubbed faces, and chose to express a candour none of us was accustomed to from Indian officialdom. 'I look at you all,' he said bluntly, 'the best and the brightest of our fair land, smart, honest and able, and my heart sinks. Because I know that most of you will do what I did and take the civil service examinations, little realizing that if you succeed, your fate will be to take orders from the dregs of our society—the politicians.' He could see the shock on the faces of his audience as he went on, 'Don't make the mistake I did. Do something else with your lives.'

Yes, it was none other than the inimitable Natwar Singh. I have never forgotten the speech, thinking about which kept me awake most of that night—and helped change my own career plans. If someone as successful and important in the bureaucracy as Natwar Singh could feel this way, I wondered, what satisfaction could ordinary people without his rank or connections derive from government service? Of course, Natwar went on to put his money where his mouth was: he resigned from the government before he could attain the foreign secretaryship, which most of his peers considered inevitable, and entered politics instead. This gave him a stint as minister of state and then minister for external affairs, where he could give orders to the foreign secretary of the day. I am sure he relished the opportunity to set standards of which the 'dregs of society' were incapable.

I didn't take the Foreign Service exams that all my contemporaries expected me to ace; instead, I joined the UN—and years later, when the opportunity arose, joined Natwar's 'dregs of society' myself.

Contributing to the Idea of India

Three years is, of course, a small—and rapidly decreasing—proportion of my life, but my three years at St. Stephen's College, DU, marked me for all the years to follow. Partly, this was because I joined college a few months after my sixteenth birthday and left it a few months after my nineteenth, so I was at St. Stephen's at an age when any experience would have had a lasting effect. But equally vital was the institution itself, its atmosphere and history, its student body and teaching staff, its sense of itself and how that sense was communicated to each individual character. Too many Indian colleges are places for lectures, rote-learning, memorizing, regurgitation; St. Stephen's encouraged random reading, individual note-taking, personal tutorials and extracurricular development. Elsewhere, you learned to answer the questions, at St. Stephen's, to question the answers. Some of us went further and questioned the questions.

Standing in the college premises on its 125th birthday, I remembered the values the institution had taught me, in the classroom and outside it. St. Stephen's influenced me fundamentally, gave me my basic faith in all-inclusive, multi-spirited and free-thinking cultures; helped shape my mind and define my sense of myself in relation to the world and so, inevitably, influenced what I have done later in life—as a man, as a UN official, as a writer and, now, as a politician. Stephania encouraged the development of qualities that would stand me in good stead in each of these activities.

The great humanist and Stephanian Gopalkrishna D. Gandhi summarized the qualities of Stephania in the Urdu word *tahzib*. In a speech at the college in 2009, he went on to explain:

> *To seek opportunity but not be an opportunist,*
> *To make one's money but not rake it in,*
> *To look for a 'shaabbaash' but not chase after popularity,*
> *To advance without flattery,*
> *To retreat without abandoning,*
> *To offer loyalty but not cronyism,*
> *To make a point without wanting to win the argument,*
> *To make an impression without wanting to leave a mark,*
> *To make a difference without wanting to be hailed as a Prophet,*
> *Is to have tahzib.*

To work for success rather than for victory,
And never to want to flash that revolting two-finger sign mimicking the letter 'V',
Is to have tahzib.

So, when I look back at DU today, I celebrate the secularism, the pan-Indian outlook, the well-rounded education, the eclectic social interests, the questioning spirit and the meritocratic culture that are the vital ingredients of the Stephanian ethos. These are what the idea of Stephania contributes to the idea of India I have described in my books and speeches around the world. DU peers who were heirs to this ethos are, in this centenary year, the 'Men of the Year'—indeed, of any year.

A TRYST WITH ECONOMICS AND LAW

Dhananjaya Y. Chandrachud

Since its founding movement a century ago, Delhi University has expanded its reach and grasp well beyond its four initial colleges. In doing so, it has accepted and nurtured students across the country and the world, embellishing its reputation of being an inclusive institution. Beyond its vibrant academic programmes, the university nurtures a distinctive ethos and culture. It has stimulated an environment for dialogue and debate, adding heft to its core foundation with each passing decade.

My tryst with DU began in July 1976, just about a year after the declaration of national Emergency on 25 June 1975. Travelling to the university in the ubiquitous DTC routes 210, 220 and 240 from Central Secretariat, a young student could not miss the placards at the bus stops. The initial atmosphere at the university was hushed, and political debates were clamped down. But despite these curbs on debate, there were vibrant meetings and gatherings. These meetings set the tone for a society founded on the core values of liberty and free speech. Ragging had been officially banned; what remained of it as we entered the portals of the university were relics of what it meant to be ragged a few years ago.

I joined St. Stephen's College to pursue the Bachelor of Arts programme with an honours degree in economics. The college had admitted me initially for the degree course in History Honours. But my dreams lay elsewhere. In the course of the interview—the panel was chaired by Principal W.S. Rajpal—the faculty voiced its scepticism about my ability to pursue economics, which required a strong foundation in mathematics. I was admitted to the Economics Honours degree programme and took mathematics as my subsidiary subject in the hope that it would lay the foundation for a specialization in economics. Instead of choosing philosophy as a subsidiary subject in the first year, as most of my batchmates did, I took up Hindi and thoroughly enjoyed traversing the literary works of eminent authors and poets.

Thirty-eight years later, as Chief Justice of the Allahabad High Court, I realized how important the engagement with Hindi is for a person like me, whose childhood was spent in Mumbai. In the six years of university life, I acquired much of the colloquial Hindi prevalent at the time. The works of Mahadevi Verma, Munshi Premchand and Ramnaresh Tripathi left a deep impact on us. Our time at the university equipped us to step into the world. Our peers were bright stars on the horizon, and we looked up to them for their brilliance. They inspired us to do better.

As one of DU's founding colleges, St. Stephen's of our day laid emphasis on maintaining a high standard of academics. Our education taught us about the schools of economic thought as well as about structures of governance. There was an outstanding faculty at the Department of Economics, comprising, amongst others, professors Kalyanjit Roy Choudhury, who taught microeconomics; Dinkar Khullar, who taught us macroeconomics; R.C. Malhan, who taught national income and accounting; and the irrepressible Vinod Chowdhury, whose lectures on the Indian economy were spliced with his impeccable command of English. Pedagogy at St. Stephen's included lectures as well as tutorials. I have fond memories of lectures held on the manicured lawns of the campus, especially in the winter months of Delhi.

The winds of change that would sweep the nation after the declaration of election results in 1977 found resonance in college life. Sprawled on the lawns of the campus, we would discuss problems of India and the world, all of which seemed to rest on our shoulders. We had gratuitous solutions at our fingertips. Life was simple and so were our solutions.

St. Stephen's kindled a strong work ethic. While classes took up the first part of the day, a few library enthusiasts like me would continue to work in the campus, catching a late evening DTC bus to head home. During the decade of the 1970s, the college was regarded as a nursery for civil services, comprising some of the brightest young minds. True to the college's reputation, the students in my cohort established themselves in the field of public administration as parliamentarians and academics. The Emergency years spawned a generation of young leaders who were to leave the college to join politics in the quest of a better future for the nation.

However, it would be remiss to suggest that life in St. Stephen's was restricted to academics. There was the joy of campus life, be it while visiting the Tibetan market—'Tib Dabs' at Majnu Ka Tila—savouring a scrambled egg on toast in the college canteen, guzzling gallons of nimboo paani while discussing Paul Samuelson or William Baumol, or simply watching an intercollegiate cricket match.

Into a Melting Pot

After graduating at the first position in first class from St. Stephen's, I decided to pursue a master's degree in economics from the Delhi School of Economics (DSE). Since classes were due to start in a few weeks, I began attending lectures at the Campus Law Centre (CLC). I was captivated by law and by the way it was taught by our teachers. They intertwined questions of policy and constitutional morality with the quest for liberty and freedom. A few lectures at CLC led me to make the career-altering choice of pursing an LLB degree.

Legal education in India, at the time, was restricted to a handful of centres of excellence. Besides CLC of DU, there were other institutions of prominence, such as the Government Law College (GLC) in Mumbai and the Indian Law Society's (ILS) Law College in Pune. The study of law as a serious academic discipline was yet to spread across the nation. Inspired by Professor N.R. Madhava Menon, the national law schools were yet to arrive on the scene. DU, therefore, became a hub and centre, attracting students from all parts of the country where quality legal education was not available. Their presence brought diversity and plural values, which nourished not only the students but the faculty at the university as well. While the university has shaped the lives of those who have entered its portals, students, in turn, have shaped the university into becoming the body that it is today.

The distinguishing feature of studies at CLC was its pedagogy. Adopting the case method propounded by Christopher Columbus Langdell, dean of Harvard Law School, the teaching of law at the university required students to learn the law by reading, analysing and critiquing judicial decisions. Through this process, we were encouraged to look beyond the letter of the law to understand the social, historical and political context in which the law has evolved, and the vision of society that the law seeks to attain.

My learning at CLC has been instrumental in shaping my views as a lawyer and, later, as a judge. I recall the lectures of Dr Lotika Sarkar, who taught us criminology. She became our mentor in understanding human rights, the feminist movement and gender studies. Dr B. Sivarammiah was an erudite scholar on law and poverty. Dr B. Erabby was brilliance personified in his understated eloquence on constitutional jurisprudence. I cherish my interactions with Professor Upendra Baxi, who had an office at CLC. His copious notes while editing my article titled 'Evolving Trends in Locus Standi: Models for

Decision Making' imparted a lifelong experience in writing and editing.

Life at CLC was in stark contrast to that at Stephen's. While the latter provided an insulated environment and allowed for theoretical learning of the subject, the former was a microcosm of society, reflecting its diversity and its real-world issues, and provided a practical learning experience. The students at CLC came from all corners of the country. As a Maharashtrian born and brought up in Mumbai and Delhi, I had a chance to share the culture, diversity and stories of persons from different walks of life at the university.

In many ways, CLC was a melting pot of religions, classes and regions. The students at CLC, all of whom had completed three years of undergraduate studies, reflected a certain level of maturity, nurturing the academic environment. The personal backgrounds of students allowed for discussions on the law and its intersection with social and political sciences, and economics and philosophy, among others. CLC has produced doyens of the Bar and several judges of the Supreme Court and high courts. It is unique that four of us from the same batch—justice(s) Sanjay Kishan Kaul, S. Ravindra Bhat, Hrishikesh Roy and myself—find ourselves serving the same institution together four decades later!

Beyond the Letter of the Law

Much has changed in the legal landscape after the revolution in legal education in the 1990s. We have seen the growth of national law universities and other private and government universities, making the study of law more accessible. The law degree has now been transformed from a three-year programme to a five-year integrated programme. The degree now is not only integrated with the study of social sciences but, increasingly, law schools offer an intersection of the law degree with management subjects and core science majors—all of which undoubtedly play a role in developing the perspective of a student.

Law schools have adopted a realistic approach to familiarize students with the practice of law through the introduction of internships during the term, participation in mock courtroom simulations, mediation competitions and client counselling sessions, among others. The plethora of activities that a law student can participate in during their studies allows them to make an informed decision regarding their future career path.

At the same time, however, institutions such as CLC, GLC Mumbai and ILS Pune remain committed to the idea of a three-year law degree after undergraduate studies. While an integrated programme has served the needs of the industry, particularly the corporate sector, there is merit to the continuation of the three-year law degree. However, the latter should also look to the future and reinvent its academic programme to accommodate subject choices of students during law school. For instance, CLC can use its position within DU for allowing cross-registration of courses with other faculties and departments. Similarly, students in their undergraduate programmes at DU can opt for subjects at the CLC, specifically those relating to their profession, and get a glimpse into law as a career option. Such initiatives would increase the opportunities for students of DU and bring the university in line with law schools abroad.

Albert Einstein said that 'Education is not the learning of many facts but the training of the mind to think.' In my experience, DU equips one not just with the ability to think but also trains one for situations that life offers outside of the university. DU has enabled us as students to learn the law, but it did much beyond that—the university and its vibrant environment enabled us to think about the law. In thinking about the law, we, as students, were initiated into our first understanding of the relationship of law and society.

DU is truly a national treasure. I am proud to call it my alma mater. Each day provides us with a reason to relive what I learnt as a student of the university. Our continuing association provides a humbling awareness of the responsibility that each generation bears towards creating a just, compassionate and humane future.

DAKSHINAMURTY: NOTES FROM THE SOUTH AND FEMINIST LEGACY

Lakshmi Puri

बीजस्यान्तरिवाङ्कुरो जगदिदं प्राङ निर्विकल्पं पुनः
माया कल्पित देश काल कलना वैचित्र्य चित्रिकृतम्
मायावीव विजृम्भयत्यपि महायोगीव यः
स्वेच्छया तस्मै श्री गुरु मूर्तये नम इदं श्रीदक्षिणामूर्तय

Obeisance to him, Shri Dakshinamurty, who is the Guru, who, out of his free will, like the magician or a great yogi, manifests this world, which was before creation, undifferentiated even as the sprout was within the seed and became variegated later on in contact with space and time, brought forth by Maya!

For me—Murdeshwar by birth—Delhi University, my college Lady Shri Ram College (LSR), and later, the then newly opened South Campus has been an experience as immersive as Shiva Dakshinamurthy, or the south-facing Shiva. It magically manifested a whole new and variegated world to me, transformed me and provided me with the space to explore my power of possibility at the time of the greatest promise. I will always remain grateful for those rites of passage that I passed through at LSR to emerge into my personhood and identity.

Thumbing through the pages of the book of my life, and going back and forth, I have realized that some major diversions, disruptions and thwarting of original purposes happen for a reason. Life, like history, makes us go through what T.S. Eliot called 'cunning passages' and 'contrived corridors', and throws up issues that deceive with 'whispering ambitions'.[1]

The decision to join LSR was, in many ways, the sort of unanticipated destiny that Eliot was referring to. I was a surprise *shendephal* (youngest child)—the last of three daughters born to 45-year-old parents—who was privileged to be pampered excessively by her family. I later discovered there was another side to that privilege after I had finished my schooling. Around that time, my father had retired as Law Secretary from the government with no assets, save his pension, to fall back on.

He had begun a practice at the Supreme Court, but it was uncertain terrain. Despite the lack of financial clarity, my family encouraged me to pursue a professional career in my own right. This was the result of growing up with feminist parents who wanted me to fulfil my aspirations. My mother, in particular, nurtured in me the dream of becoming a doctor—just like

[1]Eliot, T.S., 'Gerontion'.

the gynaecologist Dr Pasricha at the Wellington Hospital she deified because of the miracle 'live-or-die' caesarean operation that the doctor performed to save us both.

I had deliberately pursued the Science stream in my school, Mater Dei, and won a Science Talent scholarship in the hopes of studying biochemistry—my favourite subject—in college. After looking at the limited career alternatives that STEM studies provided at the time in either teaching or government research labs, I went ahead and secured admission in the pre-med course at Dayal Singh College of DU. To fulfil my mother's and my own aspiration, my father went along with it.

However, on the day I received my pre-med admission, he said to me that he had had an epiphany about something extraordinary I could aspire to. And on a more pragmatic level, since my career as a doctor would take eight long years—and then a few more years to settle into the profession—before it could take off, he was not sure he could support me with a legal practice he had just embarked upon.

He also argued that I would be hard-put to follow my passion for Bharatanatyam, and English and Marathi literature simultaneously with the rigorous studying and extreme hard work that medical studies required; or when I marry and have a family, to find the right work–life balance.

'So, Dada, do you want me to forego the opportunity to be an Indian woman in science or to serve the country by joining the noblest profession on earth—that of a doctor?' I asked, quite frustrated with the force of his logic, which was always served up on a gentle persuasive platter that I could rarely resist.

'Look, if you still decide that you want to be a doctor or scientist, I will do my best to support you. But first consider the alternative plan. Why don't you serve the country as an Indian Foreign Service (IFS) officer and represent India abroad? There are so few Indian women in diplomacy. You are well-suited for that role. That would be a short four-year trajectory. The best route is your doing BA History Honours—you can join the Lady Shri Ram College in South Delhi, which is close to us here in Green Park, and then the moment you are eligible, appear for the civil services exam without even waiting to finish your MA. Oh yes, remember that to get the IFS allotment, you must be among the first 15 in rank,' he replied, flashing a dimpled smile to make these impossible targets appear like a breeze.

Brought up to think and decide for myself, I debated the options long and hard. I was tempted by the prospect he set out for me. As a child, I had seen him as a respected and well-loved legal advisor to His Majesty the King of Nepal, helping even in drafting Nepal's first constitution, just as he had been part of Babasaheb's team in the making of India's constitution. I had been fascinated by the power and influence of the Indian embassy there, and the wide scope of work of the Indian Aid Mission. So, I convinced myself that my father's plan must become my destiny.

That Can-Do Spirit

Was I being a *jeune fille rangee*—a dutiful daughter—that Simone de Beauvoir, the existentialist philosopher and feminist, wrote about or was I exercising my agency that she and my father had ignited in me? Whatever it was, I diverged sharply into the humanities, in the History Honours track, never to look back at the STEM path. That is how I joined LSR—a premier women's college in DU that had started rivalling the older Miranda House my elder sister Indira had attended, in academics as well as extracurricular endeavours.

There were some things missing—the hustle, especially in competition with young men, the animal energy of inter-college competitions, the raging *dangals* of myriad hues, and the cut-and-thrust of Kautilya-inspired student politics of the established campus of the DU, which was many Bus Specials away.

My decision meant that I was in another all-female universe of learning—almost confirming my fate of 'growing up a nun' through school and college, as my daughters later used to joke with me when I dared to offer dating advice to them. It kept me away from meeting a brilliant, dashing someone, a mover and shaker, in Hindu College, in North Campus. He was to be revealed to me only later, when I joined the IFS, as my love and soulmate for *saat janam* (seven lives)!

There is something to be said for being in an all-women college environment, whatever the downside. For one, gender equality is not a contested idea. For most of us, learning was an empowering journey. The majority of my college-mates were competitive young women fired by the ambition to take up exciting careers, driven partly by their own will but also equally by a generation of frustrated, educated mothers like mine who had sacrificed their careers to instead raise their families. There were also those who were simply seeking education for enlightenment ahead of marriage and to have a good time. We also had girls who were the first in their family to attend college and eagerly lapped up everything college had to offer.

Many like me were heady with ideas of the global feminist movement, the second wave of which was coursing through the United States (US) and Europe, and filtering through to educational campuses in Indian cities.

My father had gifted me Simone de Beauvoir's book *The Second Sex* for my fifteenth birthday. It was described as a revolutionary and incendiary attempt to confront history from a feminist perspective and an act of Promethean audacity—a theft of Olympian fire—that was to irreversibly transform the way women and men looked at themselves and their relationship with each other and the world.

Though patriarchy continued to reign in so many domains in India, even more than the West, I was deeply influenced by the book's messages to find gender-positive references in one's own tradition. In my own reflections after reading the book, I discovered hundreds of such symbols and customs in my own cultural heritage, including most notably the Ardhanarishwara (the half-man, half-woman form of Shiva) or devi worship.

Growing up in a household of only daughters, we never felt as the 'other', defined exclusively in opposition to men. We were never denied our humanity. Nor did we ever feel that we were not playing the role of the Self or Subject. We learnt to see ourselves as essential, absolute and transcendent, just like Beauvoir claimed men saw themselves as, and we extended out into the world, wanting to act, invent, create and save others, not be saved by men.

My mother was among those women who were the first generation of emancipated women driving the gender discourse. She had been a pioneer in women's higher education but gave up her career after marriage. She relentlessly fired me into 'realizing my full potential', whatever that meant, and using the university as a racing track to get to the finish line of my career goals.

It was with this 'I can do anything, I can be anything' spirit that I joined LSR, coincidentally when the feminist discourse was fuelled by three path-breaking books that came out between 1970 and 1972. Both inside and outside our history, political science and psychology classrooms, the ideas of Kate Millett's bestseller *Sexual Politics*—which, when broadened, included 'power-structured' relationships, and asserted that the 'personal was political'—reverberated in our college circles and impelled us to question verities we all had grown up with in politics, literature, cinema and in real life.

The same year, Shulamith Firestone, the founder of the New York Radical Feminists (NYRF), published *The Dialectic of Sex*, making what was then a sensational claim that love disadvantaged women by creating shackles for them with their male oppressors. In 1971, in my second year of college, Germaine Greer's *The Female Eunuch* shook us all up with the thesis that sexual repression of women deprived them of the creative energy they needed to be independent and self-fulfilled.

But the one personality who fired my imagination the most was Gloria Steinem—she had lived in India and had become the most charismatic proponent of 'women's liberation', which was to become the rallying cry of our generation of women in DU. Her writings and speeches, urging young women to wage a million mutinies every day in every way to assert their equal rights, made us all brave—in our homes, in the university and in the wider world.

The *Ms.* magazine Gloria founded and wrote many iconoclastic articles in, travelled to us in elliptical ways at LSR. This, at a time, when there was no internet or social media. Ideas still had wings then and travelled like migratory birds to hospitable islands like DU, perching themselves on eager heads like mine! I picked and chose as many as possible. I could not have dreamt that decades later, I was to connect with Gloria in New York and fight together for our 'Mission Possible' of gender equality!

There were enough young women in the university who rejected the premises of the three streams of feminism—liberal feminism, radical liberalism and difference feminism. Many, however, picked and chose what sat most comfortable with their self-belief and aspirations. The sceptics of feminism in the university who often thought it was about hating men or despaired that a new normal of gender equality was not possible were shaken up enough. Even they began to join the questioning, unleashed by the feminist discourse, to challenge the gender-based division of labour in households, discrimination at the workplace, or the boy preference and girl aversion in society.

Before joining the university, our ideas of feminism were shaped by the heroines of the freedom movement and social reform icons that came to prominence. The pantheon included Rani Lakshmibai, Ahilyabai Holkar, Sarojini Naidu, Savitribai Phule, Ramabai Ranade, Kamaladevi Chattopadhyay, Pupul Jayakar, Vijaya Lakshmi Pandit (who was the first woman president of the UNGA and diplomat par excellence) and Prime Minister Indira Gandhi. Indira ji showed that she could beat any man at statecraft and was a powerful yet strategic wartime leader who sculpted the 1971 victory against Pakistan, giving birth to Bangladesh. She inspired and empowered young women in DU as a modern-day incarnation of Durga.

The self-belief that Durga resides in every one of us Indian girls and women grew exponentially in those days. From this seminal churning in LSR on woman power arose a multitude of freethinking, bold and ahead-of-their-times women who were determined to carve their own place in the world. LSR can boast of a bevy of women who made their mark in politics, business, theatre, journalism, media, literature, art, music, dance, films, diplomacy, education and international institutions through the 1970s up to now.

A Nourishing Milieu

From having the image of a college come-lately begetting nerds at best to behanjis at worst, LSR assumed a pride of place by combining a reputation for academic excellence and topping university exams. It 'produced' women who broke the shackles of patriarchy by embracing modernity, cultivated a scientific temper, sought independence, and self-realization—often supported by Indian civilizational traditions. No wonder then that the matrimonial ads of those years in newspapers asking for 'Fair, wheat-complexioned girl from well-to-do families, caste no bar' took pains to rule out the feminist rebels bred by our college by stipulating 'LSR girls need not apply!' What a badge of honour!

I wonder what would have happened had I not gone to this part of the university—would I have been as well-prepared for a role I was destined to play four decades later? And would I later play a leading role in founding and building the first-ever global organization to promote gender equality and women's empowerment, UN Women, from the ground up?

UN Women today, I am proud to say, is a veritable wellspring of feminist thinking and mainstreaming, of establishing international norms and standards for gender equality, and of advocacy and movement-building in the feminist domains. It will remain my most significant contribution—and as I write this piece, I realize that apart from my parents, it was my education and feminist awakening in LSR that have made this possible.

With the benefit of hindsight, I can say that the buildings, facilities, equipment and organization that universities provide, the curriculum they offer and the stage they set for extracurricular activities are important markers of excellence. Even though the culture and ethos of an institution may assume a greater meaning than the sum of its tangible parts, it is essential that the underlying framework provide its inhabitants with the best possible tools and resources. Our principal, Dr Luthra, ran the college wonderfully in these respects, and many of our departments achieved the reputation of being among the best in DU as we shone in sports, drama, dance and debating.

Similarly, without the kind of excellence in teaching and creative space that LSR provided, my story of becoming the youngest IFS entrant—at first attempt, besides—and the achievement of standing second in the All India Civil Services Exam, that too immediately after BA History Honours, would not have been inscribed in my Book of Life. Needless to say, my destiny was as much the brainchild of my father as it was of the nourishing milieu of LSR in which I was able to build the tools to achieve my—and his—dream.

If I were to identify one single factor that made a difference to what made me flourish, it was the quality of the faculty. I aver now that universities are as good as its professors, who are not only founts of knowledge and wisdom, exuding and instilling excitement about learning, but also act as bridges to the outside world of ideas, enterprise and reality even as they keep revitalizing themselves with new and potent concepts that whirl around.

One of our professors, Surjit Mansingh, was a lodestar in my professional ambitions coming to fruition. A former IFS officer who had to resign because she married a foreigner, she became an academic in the US and came back to teach at DU. A feminist, she became my intellectual inspiration, philosopher and guide.

Surjit and I developed a particularly close, latter-day guru–shishya relationship, in which we both interrogated each other and constantly engaged in bouts of *shastrarth* (debate) on topics ranging from Hinduism to Indian incarnation of feminism, and how they were different from their western counterparts. She introduced me to the intricacies of international relations, law, foreign policy and diplomacy, which helped me not only pass the IFS exams but also in my diplomatic profession throughout.

Another inspiring teacher was Kunku Soota, a topper from SOAS University, London, and a young, vibrant and brilliant teacher who stoked our passion about deciphering the past to draw lessons for our present and our future. She made us heady with the thought of reimagining our identity as liberated young women. She arranged for us to visit historical monuments in Rajasthan, Agra and Khajuraho, to feel the vibrations of history in stone, rubble and the earth on which they stood centuries later, and engage with settlements around them!

Each one of our teachers, viz. Ms Madhok, Ms Kunj Gupta, Ms Kamala Gupta, et al., took personal interest in our intellectual growth as well as our grasp of their subjects, and how we fared at the yearly exams. I remember when I missed a first division in my second-year exams, some of my teachers expressed astonishment and encouraged me to course-correct and secure a first division in my final BA exam—which I did.

In the newly opened South Campus of DU, in a building near the nala in South Extension Part 1 (which I had joined for my MA History), I was blessed to have some of the best and original brains as my teachers, including the eccentric ones—those I especially bonded with. Years later, in 2002, as director in the United Nations Conference on Trade and Development (UNCTAD), an intergovernmental organization and think tank to promote the economic growth and development of developing countries of the Global South, I revelled in being accused of driving an 'Eccentric University of the South'. This appellation was for divining and advocating robust alternative models and 'pie in the sky' economic development theories defying prevailing northern wisdom.

A Thousand Flowers Bloom

The history of India, including under the British rule, which was hitherto written mostly by British historians, had begun to be written by, for and of Indians. But as can be expected, a thousand flowers bloomed as ideological orientations. There began the tussle between the Left and the nationalist interpretation of history. Our minds were opened by professors of both persuasions.

We got to engage in formal and informal debates on the greatness of our Hindu civilization, which, century after century, tragically succumbed to foreign rule. We studied how alien, assimilated or benevolent each of our foreign rulers were. How we could reclaim our past glory while building a new, composite, united and prosperous India was the crux of our discourse, and multiple political ideologies led us to different answers in true Vedic tradition of '*ekam sad vipra bahudha vadanti agnim yamam matariswanam ahuh* (truth is one but the learned refer to it by different names)!'

So, it was with this interpretation of our history—at times turbulent, at times edifying—as a civilization and as a country that I broadened my horizons for learning in college. Within these criteria, I was interested in applying the feminist lens and its peculiar intersectional ties in the Indian context.

The idea of India, particularly in the context of who we are in relation to our colonial past, was redefined in our generation that was born after Independence and came of age in the early 1970s. DU was a crucible for developing that idea. By then, revelations about the Harappa and Mohenjo-Daro remains had astounded the world about the sophisticated and evolved Indus Valley civilization. We were proud heirs to one of the oldest civilizations and to a many-splendoured composite culture. What achievements the civilization represented in building empires of brick and stone but also of culture, humanism and spiritualism pan-India and beyond! Despite successive invasions in the medieval period, I am amazed that we were able to retain our identity and cultural integrity while absorbing new influences. We celebrated the nationalist resurgence under the Marathas and the Sikhs. We better understood why a country of India's size, population and means caved under British assault—disunity being the main reason.

We rejoiced at the legacy of our freedom struggle and made the teachings of Mahatma Gandhi a part of our intellectual and spiritual make-up as Indians and as citizens of the world. That I represent not just a country of subcontinental proportions but one of the richest, oldest and profoundest civilizations made me hold my head high in representing India in foreign countries and at the United Nations (UN). The beauty and unity in diversity of the Indian people and their culture was demonstrated and lived every day among the boarders, day scholars and teachers at LSR—which was a microcosm of the churn in India in the 1970s—who came from different states, classes, caste, creed and backgrounds, and even foreign countries.

We became so fused as a new generation of young Indian women coming together to carve out our own new paths that we scarcely noticed our differences. The idea of India and being an Indian was also celebrated in classrooms and in the plethora of activities the college encouraged—drama, debating, sports, dance, poetry and much else. Many of us joined the National Social Service (NSS) to serve the poor and disadvantaged.

LSR's Sanskrit department was as strong as its English department, and our study of Indian history covered all periods and also the interplay with the Far East, Europe and the Americas. As Mahatma Gandhi had taught us, we in LSR were strongly rooted in Indian thought and yet 'kept our windows open' for ideational winds from everywhere in the world to come blowing in to enlighten us all.

During the 1971 Indo-Pak war and its aftermath, the college, as much as DU, was imbued with a marvellous spirit of patriotism—bred as much by air-raid sirens, blackouts, curfews and hiding in bunkers that signalled a nation in peril as by the heroism, sacrifice and ultimate success of our armed forces and political leadership in winning a just war. The college encouraged us all to do our bit to support our jawans. I have vivid memories of collecting money to donate for their welfare, and handing food and money over to their commanding officers in trains headed for the frontier. In between classes, the front lawns of LSR became mass camps for knitting sweaters and mufflers for our brave soldiers fighting on the cold northern frontiers. Patriotism assumed a new urgency and meaning.

We practised, and avidly watched and listened to all forms of Indian classical dance and music. But we loved and sang folk and Hindi film songs and western pop songs in our antakshari sessions in college. We listened to *Binaca Geetmala* and to All India Radio's *Yuva Bharati* broadcast of English songs, including The Beatles, Cliff Richard and Elvis Presley, among others. I was among those who could quote Sanskrit slokas, Marathi poems of Maydeva and Yashwant, Punjabi tappas, Kabir's dohas, verses from Jaishanker Prasad's *Kamayani*, Sarojini Naidu's 'Palanquin

Bearers', Shakespeare and Wordsworth's sonnets, and Gurudev Tagore's Rabindra Sangeet.

We were a curious blend of tradition and modernity even in our sense of attire. From the first year on, I made it a point to wear handloom cotton saris to college, including the quintessential Gujarati style, and set a trend. We wore khadi kurtas as a statement, making it 'cool' with pants and jeans. I did not demur at wearing mini-skirts or shorts while playing tennis! We were bold enough to fight back eve-teasing by those we called 'Road Romeos'—who accosted us just outside the college or around South Campus premises—sometimes embarrassing them by teasing back, and at other times, brandishing our tennis racquets!

Transformative Moulding at the Foundry

At the university, I drank a heady brew of feminism with family values; nationalism with globalism; a sense of history with an eye to the future; representing a civilizational country with an ambition for it to emerge as a great power; and clarity of thought with the ballast of rhetoric—all these held me in good stead as I battled patriarchy, prejudice, racism and the arrogance of power on the part of the different actors that I encountered in the theatre of diplomacy. The university made me fit for purpose, yes, but it also prepared me for survival as the fittest!

In my long career in the diplomatic and development world, I have encountered many complex and challenging assignments. Whether it was successfully seizing and discharging the role of a media officer in our embassy in patriarchal Japan; or being a tough negotiator as Under Secretary (Pakistan) in the Ministry of External Affairs at the risk of being labelled a hawk and left out of key events by the Government of Pakistan in sexist retaliation; or being spokesman for the Government of India and undertaking human rights work during the turbulence of the Indo-Sri Lanka Peace Accord and the Indian Peace Keeping Force operations at the cost of receiving threats from both Sinhala and Tamil extremists, even as the western press gleefully called it India's Vietnam, being innovative in exponentially growing and diversifying the Indo-Hungarian partnership from a small base—I was able to deal with these dynamic situations with confidence and dexterity because of my fearless upbringing at home and intrepid education at the university. I contributed to giving a new thrust and definition to India's economic diplomacy, including through its Look East policy and many plurilateral regional, subregional and interregional economic agreements.

As I moved on to represent India at the UN, I had to reflect national positions but also push the frontiers of progress. While I was in leadership positions in different UN organizations, the qualities of analytical temperament, responsiveness, preparedness, mental stamina and consensus-building skills and derring-do, learned over many thought-provoking conversations and lessons at DU, again held me in good stead. It helped me participate productively in contentious but intellectually stimulating and path-breaking multilateral negotiations and advocacy on UN conventions, treaties, norms and standards.

I was instrumental in convening the first-ever history-making Global Summit on Gender Equality in 2015, with 70 heads of state attending and pledging their commitment. Even as I advanced the national economic agenda forward at various platforms, I continued to be a leading advocate and exemplar for multicultural UN management teams in different organizations. In many ways, what I had to deal with at university, as we women were beginning to make a mark, was similar to my experiences at the UN, where despite pushback and often searing competition and power play, I learned to cultivate the fungibility of a specialist-generalist to make my stand and my country's effectively. I was, thus, able to contribute my mite to humanities' projects of peace and security, sustainable development, human rights and humanitarian action.

I owe much of who I became and who I am today to the transformative moulding I underwent for four years at the foundry of the DU. It is my ardent wish that the university becomes the locus of revitalizing—nay reinventing and future-forwarding—higher education in India so that we become an *Aatmanirbhar*, *Shikshit*, *Sakushal* and *Shreshtha Bharat* that continues to drink the amrit of India's great spiritual, cultural and intellectual heritage. It must stoke and generate woman power like never before. It must contribute to our ideal of every Indian youth getting access to and benefitting from quality university education so that no young man or woman is left behind or is forced to go abroad in its quest.

It is my hope that our vishvavidyalayas (universities), as 'Centres of Excellence' in this Indian century, led by the central node of DU, should generate global talent reservoirs and become the chakras for the Tech Economy 4.0 that will spawn innovative social, economic and political projects. We will then be able to re-establish our rightful place as a 'Vishwa Guru'. Into that heaven of knowledge, let my country now awake!

OF BUSES, THEATRICS AND A DISOBEDIENT SPIRIT

Imtiaz Ali

I never bought a bus ticket in the three years I was a student at Delhi University even though I only travelled by buses in those days. This disobedience was an ethic of DU that all hostellers had to uphold in my day. We were told by our seniors to not buy bus tickets. So, I stood in buses like a gangster, and on the rare occasion of being asked by the lazy conductor, said 'Student' and gave him tough looks.

Now, there was a myth in Delhi that a university student had a fight with the bus staff on a ride one day. He was beaten up. Then the fight ended, the journey resumed, and towards the end of it, the bus entered DU. Here, the student stopped the bus and called his friends, who not only beat up the staff in return but also set the bus on fire. It was on the power of this myth that I pulled my free bus rides in Delhi. I did not know if this story was true, but neither did the bus conductor. I am grateful that in three years I was never challenged to call my friends and burn a bus—that would never have worked.

But more than that I am thankful that this privilege forced me to grow up in ways that are possible only in DU. I didn't turn out to be a gangster, no one did; I just became a man of the world. To break the rule was the first rule in order to thrive in DU in my time. Strange as it may sound, the establishment seemed to favour the anti-establishment voice.

I had made it a habit to show up at the office and residence of P.C. Verma, the principal of Hindu College during my time—often without notice—to ask for one thing or the other for the first theatre play I did in college. Mr Verma was neither friendly nor did he ever brush me off. And yet, one day, he said those golden words that impacted my life more than anything else at the university: 'Don't waste your time attending classes. I will sign your attendance register, and you will be allowed to take the exam. In return, you will have to do two theatre productions for the college every year.' I immediately agreed, sold my soul to the devil and plunged headlong into theatre. The theatre group we formed during my first year in college—Ibtida—began buzzing with activity. Thirty-two years later, it is still buzzing with activity. I directed more than two productions for the college each year and was involved in theatre plays with Miranda House and Indraprastha (IP) College as well (more on that later). I joined a theatre group called Act One in Mandi House as well, and Mr Verma made sure I was allowed to take the exams all three years.

Now that I look back on all that transpired, I wonder how wrong it was that a principal should say such a thing to a student. I couldn't believe it, especially because he was a teacher in my department. Needless to say, I did not attend a single lecture of his in three years. But I also wonder about how right he was. He saw me, he must have seen the likes of me before, he recognized my trajectory and he set me free. This 'turning toward myself', as Rumi says, saved me. It is difficult to calculate the influence of that statement on my career. That is vision. And these are the kinds of people one met in DU. They were not teaching moral science from a school book. These gentlemen were telling you that school was over now, get serious.

Anyway, from what I remember, there used to be only one theatre group in a college during my time in the 1990s. Being somewhat in touch with DU theatre groups, I realize that now there are multiple theatre groups in each college. In Hindu College, for instance, there is an English theatre society, a Hindi theatre group and Ibtida, which is chiefly a street theatre society. There might even be more theatre groups in colleges today. Back in the day, there was only Ibtida, which performed proscenium as well as street plays. Before Ibtida, the chance to perform plays chiefly came along during the various college festivals. All colleges hosted festivals, and those were days of great confluence and fun. One of the prestigious and highly contested events, regardless of the festival, was the drama competition. The usual suspects at such events were St. Stephen's College, Hindu College, Kirori Mal College (KMC), Shri Ram College of Commerce (SRCC), Ramjas College, Hansraj College, sometimes Shri Guru Tegh Bahadur

Khalsa College, and the slightly disadvantaged Miranda House, IP College, Daulat Ram College and Lady Shri Ram College (LSR) for being all-women colleges.

Right to Disobedience

I remember my first time on stage in DU. It was at a festival in KMC. Roshan Abbas, in his third year then, was directing the play, and I, a green-faced fresher or *fachcha*, was acting. The play was self-written and was called *Ajayab Ghar*. In the play, I remember that I was supposed to be given an injection that woke me up in pain; I was supposed to scream in pain and then proceed to the front stage to deliver a powerful soliloquy. My seniors, Shantanu Srivastav and Shantanu Sinha, were on stage with me and so was Roshan, in a freeze, in the middle of the stage. During the show, when this injection was given to me and I screamed in pain, the audience booed and catcalled in response because they found something effeminate—I presume—in that scream. (This booing was fair game because all colleges jeered the performances of other colleges to demoralize the actors and spoil their performance. Everyone did this, including us, and in retrospect, I think this provided great training to the players to keep their act tight.)

After my scream, I had to cross to the front stage to deliver the speech to an unruly audience that was waiting to devour me. As I crossed the frozen Roshan to go up, he muttered under his breath, 'Just F*** them, Imtiaz.' I reached my mark and belted my performance with so much attitude and controlled rage that the audience had no choice but to fall silent. Overall, the play did not do too well that day, but I understood what the target audience of my plays in DU was going to be for the next three years. By the way, the audience of one's own college was no better than others. In fact, it was worse. Over the years, I performed many times on the Hindu College stage, and that was the toughest audience I have ever faced in my life. Strangely, the closest friends I had were the worst of the lot. They pointed out the vulnerabilities in the play and jeered the hell out of us. One story immediately comes to mind.

The first play performed by Ibtida was *Jati Hi Puchho Sadhu Ki*, written by Vijay Tendulkar and translated by Vasant Dev. I directed the play and also acted in it. We performed this in my first year and then again in the third year. My friends, who had seen it in the first year, came back to watch it in the third year with the knowledge that there was a romantic track in the play and scenes where I embrace a girl. Even before I embraced my co-actor, the third-year students began to create noise in anticipation. On the stage, I knew that they would bring the house down when I actually embraced her, so I hesitated and spoke some lines without embracing. My co-actor was nervous already and then also confused when I changed the 'blocking' in a running play. The lines were to be spoken in embrace, and she did not know how to justify them without it.

Following my example, she somehow managed, but it was important that the embrace happen because the scene went forward with another character 'catching us' and reacting to that. The actor who was supposed to do this was watching us from the wings, not knowing whether to even enter or not. There was nothing for him to do in that scene if we did not embrace. I could see his flabbergasted face. Recognizing this, I calculated that the embrace was a must, and I did. However, the actor who was supposed to enter hesitated because the flow of the scene was broken, and this resulted in my holding on to the embrace for much longer than needed. Suffice to say, the audience had a field day. I could feel my co-actor shivering in the embrace even as the character that was supposed to come into the scene did not so much as move a muscle. I finally called him by name and reacted as if caught by him. But over the noise of the audience, he did not hear me, and therefore, continued to wait. I had to embrace the poor girl again and scream out the name of the character loudly for him to hear and enter to catch us in the act.

From the stage, I could see my friends were having a ball of a time at our expense. They had the same right to disobedience in that audience as I had in DTC buses. As if spurred by their enjoyment and revelling in our own sudden freedom because there was nothing more to be embarrassed about, we found ourselves belting out the play shamelessly, compounding the reaction rather than cowering under the pressure. Somehow, we managed to finish the play; if ever anyone has deserved an award for a performance, it should have been for that play. I remember that one of the actors in the play, my friend Rakesh Thakur, actually blanked out on stage because of the catcalls, and he would not leave the stage when he was supposed to. Finally, he had to be pushed out by others on stage—not an easy task because he had a black belt in karate!

Going to Heaven without Dying

Two very glamourous things happened in my life while doing theatre in DU. The first was having girls from Miranda House come over to participate in a street play that I was directing. The attendance of Hindu College boys during the rehearsal of this play was, by no coincidence, high. The boys showed such dedication that many of them sat through the entire duration of each rehearsal despite not being a part of the play. However, the bonanza was that we were allowed to hold a performance inside the Miranda House premises—it was like going to heaven without dying.

The Hindu College boys could not believe that the gate outside which they had stood on numerous occasions on some false pretext or the other, was actually opened for them. We were received by a senior teacher who took us to the hostel area, and we saw swarms of girls gathering around us, cheering and catcalling in the excitement of seeing boys in their hostel for the first time. Boys would never dare to do this to girls in the university, but the girls were doing it to us. We should have been mighty happy about this, but the truth is that all of us froze. We realized that being objectified was not a compliment. It did not feel good at all. We felt shy and self-conscious. It was horrible. We managed the play somehow, but I think all of us were more sensitive to women after that.

The other glamorous event was being invited to direct a play for IP College. This was in my second year. Now, if you know DU, you are aware that by DU standards, IP was far from most colleges, including Hindu College. I had to go daily for rehearsals in the IP auditorium, but, surprisingly, I did not have problem commuting even for a single day. I did not have to take the bus either. My college friends who owned two-wheelers lined up selflessly and competed with each other to give me a ride to IP. They even insisted on staying back for the entire rehearsal to ferry me back to the hostel. So considerate were my friends in college. My brothers—so loving. One of them, whom I presently betray by taking his name, Anirudh Jakhar, even volunteered to be my assistant. I do not think he had even been inside an auditorium before—forget doing any theatre—but he promptly volunteered to assist. Really, some of those boys never ceased to amaze me for their fearless surrender to the unknown.

However, I had to leave this enterprise halfway, as I was called upon to go to Punjab with the Act One theatre group for a series of street play performances that I could not miss. I asked my friend Himanshu Tyagi to fill my shoes at IP. Himanshu not only managed to conduct the play successfully, he ended up marrying Shalini, who played one of the main roles in that play!

Back to the Warmth of the Kiln

I see so much of DU in my films. In *Rockstar* (2011), for instance, one can see a Hindu College boy walk across to St. Stephen's to propose to a girl. I have even borrowed Anirudh's surname for this character—Janardan Jakhar. If you watch the film, you will note that there is much more DU in it than just that one scene. Also, I was invited to Nirula's at Kamla Nagar for a 'Break Up Party' in my first year, and that became the basis for the story of another movie—*Love Aaj Kal* (2009). I also see in my films the spirit of revolt and protest that I saw at open debates in Jai Singh Lawn, sprouting, I suspect, from the strand of disobedience that I experienced in bus rides. DU also became my gateway to Delhi, which is personally significant because most of my films have been shot in Delhi, and many characters of my films are from Delhi.

Jai Singh and the lawn are gone now, but, in my time, he was very much serving tea inside and outside Hindu College. Jai Singh Lawn was one of those famous nooks in the university where students met to 'dispute', much like the early Athenians who we were studying in college. In these discussions, disagreement was the welcome tool to take things forward. Students came to DU from all across the country, from all social classes, and in these lawns, all people, all ideas were welcome. All thoughts were given a chance, no matter how radical they were. We sipped our tea and listened to everyone even as our preconceptions fell by the wayside.

Ideologies were formed and shattered regularly. Each time I walked out of such a discussion, I felt part of a vibrant and energetic nation.

India was served to us also in the shape of classical music performances of the highest maestros, organized by SPIC MACAY. The pleasure of listening to Pandit Hariprasad Chaurasia, Pandit Shivkumar Sharma, Ustad Zakir Hussain and many others in such intimate gatherings has eluded me ever since. It is amazing that I could access such delights so easily. Come to think of it, the impact of such evenings on impressionable students must have been sublime.

It is not going to be possible to enlist all the advantages that I and others have derived from DU, so I am not going to attempt it. Writing this was just a chance for me to go back to the warmth of the kiln that gave me some shape. The obvious facilities of a university would be present in all educational institutions constituted for the purpose, but I hold more precious the subtle manner in which DU elevated the spirits of its students. I see its lustre in all its alumni, and I hope that they see it in me too.

LEADING AND LEARNING FROM THE CHURN

Arnab Goswami

It was 1990. I had joined Delhi University after completing my Class 12 from Kendriya Vidyalaya (KV), Jabalpur. My father was in the army, so I spent most of my school years in different parts of the country, growing up in an army environment. The extended family of my parents was involved in politics in Assam, but as a student growing up in cantonments and focused almost entirely on competitive exams and the all-important board exam results, I hadn't known much of politics, leave alone seen it at close quarters.

All that changed when I entered DU at arguably the most politically volatile time. The Mandal agitation had taken hold in both the North and South campuses. At Hindu College, we prided ourselves on being actively involved in matters concerning the nation, and politics was heavy in the air. I remember being caught in a swathe of students protesting from Kranti Chowk near Ramjas College to the gates of St. Stephen's College, which had been shut and chained to keep the college out of the political protests. Our college campus was the centre of many meetings, and it was a heady feeling in those first few months on campus. Coming straight out of the insulation of home to the politics and air of dissidence in North Campus was exciting.

That summer, I decided to move in as a resident. Unable to secure a hostel seat, I joined my uncle, who was then pursuing his master's in applied geology, in the Jubilee Hall Hostel. When it became apparent that a first-year undergraduate was out of place in a postgraduate hostel, I joined a mess in Bhai Parmanand (BP) Colony, exclusively catering to students from Assam, on the other side of the road from Kingsway Camp.

They say college is about many things, and the whole college experience is measured in academic and extracurricular achievements. But if you ask me, that first year in BP Colony changed my entire approach to life. For the first time, I met students, civil service aspirants, fellow youngsters from all parts of India, from varied backgrounds and socio-economic strata, some brilliant, some tenacious, some desperate, some unsure of their career ambitions and some, as always is the case, just hanging around. But it was this range of friends and conversations that changed my perspective towards life.

My days as a student in KV had taught me the dangers of private-school elitism because I realized that true merit often emerged in the government-school environment. The tremendously competitive atmosphere at KV far outstripped the manicured setting of a private school. Every fight for the top position, rank or prize in KV was 10 times fiercer than

I had experienced earlier in a missionary school. There was contempt for privilege and respect for sheer ability.

Hindu College and DU were, for me, an extension of that spirit of competition. From being the best in my class, I was now among peers who, academically and in my chosen side career of debating, seemed better than me. My honours subject, sociology, had seemed an easy entry into UPSC preparation, but I found the diversity of the discipline baffling and tough to handle, with its emphasis on sociological theory on the one hand, and field trips to villages in Haryana by the amazing Professor P.D. Khera on the other. I lost almost all the debates I participated in during my first year, a humbling experience that probably enriched me more than I thought it did at that time. The only singular achievement, I think, in my first year was getting featured on page three of the *Hindustan Times* getting group ragged by friendly seniors on campus. It was a clipping I preserved with pride for a long time.

However, in those days, walking back from Hindu College via Hudson Lines through Mukherjee Nagar and BP Colony, the desire to win through merit, hard work and perseverance were instilled in me. I had no choice really. Topping the college was the only way to get a hostel seat, and it was pretty much a make-or-break for me. Hindu College taught me tenacity; I soaked in the atmosphere of intense effort that I saw on campus and in the hostel. Truly, I had never seen students sweat it out as much as at Hindu College. Besides that easy-going attitude during college hours there were 12-hour stretches of study from afternoon to post-midnight.

Hindu College was an oasis of UPSC and CAT rank-holders and university toppers, and I was determined to stand somewhere close to their reflected glory. The college library, with its high ceilings providing natural air conditioning, was where I spent more than 10 hours each day. Motivation levels grew in conversations with friends from humble backgrounds, hearing about their aspirations and stories. It was transformative for me at a personal level. A cliché that I hold as a life lesson—there is no substitute to hard work and struggle.

Hungry to Get Somewhere

Hostel life at Hindu College has been the breeziest period of my life. The range of interests that sprouted in every corner of the hostel was fabulous, and I made the most eclectic group of friends. Saket Shukla, pursuing Statistics Honours, now one of Delhi's top corporate lawyers, was then the most relaxed dude on the right flank. Deepak Ashish Kaul, whose addiction to ghazals only matched his unstoppable first-class grades in History Honours. Gautam Sawhney of Economics Honours, who built a reputation for calling out my last name across the flank. And Rohit Sarma of English Honours, who introduced me to Tom Petty, Roger Waters, my first cigarette and the importance of realizing that you had to 'make it' after third year. I remember Rohit (Dou as we called him) coming into my hostel room (Room 88, double sharing) one night and explaining in all seriousness that we had to 'crack' the competitive exams and 'get somewhere' after the degree.

These were great friends, and I am in touch with them even today. There was one thing common to all of them, and, in fact, across the hostel—the intensity of effort and the joy in competing. We often spoke about how we had more 'fire in our belly' than those in the insulated corridors of the college next door. And without trying to be judgmental, our life stories after college have largely matched that presumption.

Hindu College and DU built in me a practical approach to life, where all of us, more or less, concluded that privilege in youth was a recipe for disaster in later life. Little did we know that around us the country was also changing rapidly—economic liberalization had just hit, and the element of 'hunger' that we felt in us was also the mood of the country. The country was hungry for growth, and so were we.

College ended abruptly. The last four months of third year were spent slogging all day and marching down the Ridge at 2 a.m. to have anda paranthas outside Hindu Rao Hospital. I don't know what exactly it was in those anda paranthas, but the folklore around them made me believe that their nightly consumption would put you in a good consideration to top the college and university. I was broadly in that range, and so would rarely skip an opportunity. Besides, I had got, through a wildcard application, the opportunity to do my master's at Oxford, but the offer was conditional to my final-year grades, so there was no sparing of effort. I just wanted to get the unconditional offer, even though I knew that the chances of getting through a full scholarship weren't high (the scholarship offices for all top UK scholarships was in the college next door). A seat in the Delhi School of Economics was more or less assured, and I was also considering a serious shot at the civil services in 1994/1995.

I was completely shocked to see my name among those selected for the Felix Scholarship on the notice board outside the Rhodes Scholarship Office at St. Stephen's sometime around June 1993. I had never travelled abroad, and the thought of studying abroad made me cancel all D-School and MBA plans. I gave myself a treat of a rickshaw ride to Kamla Nagar and called my father. I told him they would even pay for an Air India return ticket.

Two months later, with £150 in foreign currency, a new suit stitched in Guwahati, and with my friends Dou and Deepak giving me a royal send-off, I became the first person in my family to travel abroad for a higher education at Oxford.

But truth be told, I learnt much more at DU than I did at Oxford or later at Cambridge. The biggest lesson of all was the necessity of conflict and competition between those whose families were leftovers of privileged settings during most of the twentieth century, and the possibility of changing that to a more meritocratic setting in the twenty-first century. We were the students in the 1990s, and, today, if you see the career and professional profile of those who dominate as professionals, entrepreneurs, legal luminaries and even the creative arts, you will find many who are first-generation leaders in their own right.

The 1990s was the decade that set the tone for the changes

we see in India today. Whether in our cricket team, in politics or in the media—there has been a great churn resulting in privilege being replaced by sheer merit. And I am proud to say that my generation at DU has led that churn. It is a churn necessary to take India to greatness. I have no doubt that DU and the college I am proud to call my own, Hindu College, will lead the way in that churn for the creation of a new India.

THE BEST DAYS OF MY LIFE

Raian Karanjawala

When I was asked by an old friend to collaborate with him on an anthology in honour of Delhi University, I readily agreed because, to borrow the words of a Bryan Adams song of a purported older vintage, 'those were the best days of my life.'

As I reminisced about my student life, it struck me that my first recollections were not of an academic inclination, or of the life lessons and wisdom gained. Thinking of DU takes me back, first and foremost, to the experiences I shared with a brilliant and eclectic group of students in a unique time in the history of not just the university but also of the country.

Before I delve into those heady experiences, allow me to first offer a little background that I hope shall encapsulate the atmosphere in which I was to start my studies at DU. This context also serves as the starting point for my musings, which I have divided into three interconnected parts: the politics, JP and the Emergency, and the debating culture.

Before I joined the university in 1972, it felt like India was in the ascendancy. Indira Gandhi had come out triumphant in a war against Pakistan in 1971. India had just won a test series against England in their backyard. Films of the time portrayed a sense of geniality, community and mobility. This trifecta of politics, cricket and Bollywood, which dominated the national conversation (and still does today) seemed to convey general feelings of buoyancy and spiritedness among Indians at the beginning of the 1970s.

However, as my time at DU passed, it soon became obvious that this rise was not just short-lived but also illusory. What was to follow plainly reflected India's turbulent lurches from one crisis to the next and laid bare the extent of the disaffection the common man felt towards the apathy of the 'system'. Amitabh Bachchan—who I am delighted to note has written this anthology's Foreword—probably best epitomized the frustrations of the youth through films such as *Zanjeer* (1973) and *Deewar* (1975). The 'Angry Young Man' moniker was more than just a persona; it was a powerful national archetype that resonated deeply with the country, especially its youth.

The 1970s witnessed many ruptures in India's social fabric due to the combined effects of corruption, low economic growth, high inflation, the oil crisis and the Emergency—which was the darkest period in India's experiment with democracy. In the unravelling of the established order, we saw the birth of an alternative movement that found its wings in student-led revolution. It was India's own counterculture moment, much like recent movements in other leading democracies, including, most notably, America and France. DU, naturally, was at the heart of it all.

In many ways, during my time at the university, DU felt like a microcosm of this national awakening. Amidst the education and learning, those years at DU were central in informing my politics and beliefs. And amidst the politics and bluster, those years were critical in shaping my worldview and my personality. I was privileged to have imbibed this in my three years at Shri Ram College of Commerce (SRCC) which—like its parent university—resonated with the zeitgeist. I do not think it is a matter of coincidence that some of India's most-celebrated public servants and business leaders were 'born' in that time at DU. I consider myself lucky to have been associated with a few of them.

Any such account has to be personal, and I apologize in advance for any immodesty—which you may put down to a personality trait—as well as for any inaccuracies or factual errors that are merely remnants of a poor memory and solely my responsibility.

Votes and Lifelong Friendships

When I left St. Columba's and joined SRCC in the summer of 1972, the most noticeable change was that one had left a politically agnostic—even nerdy—school to enter a culturally diverse university that was a hotbed of political activity. The politics of that time centred around one single question, namely: are you for the PM or are you against her? Incidentally, the same question underscores political discussions even today, and with almost as much heat.

Equally charged and significant in India's democratic story, I feel that the difference between the political discourse of the 1970s and today's political climate is that the debate back then was richer, more nuanced and evocative than today's vacuous polarization. But I digress. My first memory of DU is the sudden exposure to politics in the university, which, unlike school, had active youth wings of national political parties working on the ground. The Congress had the National Student Union of India (NSUI) and the Youth Congress; the Bharatiya Jana Sangh had the Akhil Bharatiya Vidyarthi Parishad (ABVP); and the socialists had the Students' Federation of India (SFI).

At the time, the politics of the university—as also of the country—roughly translated into Congress vs the rest. St. Stephen's College, and to a lesser extent, Hindu College, were representatives of the liberal school of thought, whilst SRCC, which had a 70:30 split in favour of the government schools, was the bastion of the ABVP. In hindsight, the reason is obvious, namely that while SRCC had a fair sprinkling of the Khannas and Kapurs, the predominant surnames you came across were the Aggarwals, the Jains, the Goels and the Guptas. The trader class, which these surnames symbolized, constituted the backbone of the erstwhile Jana Sangh, and it was logical that the ABVP would find electoral success in the college elections.

The outgoing college union president, Sri Ram Khanna, of the ABVP, that year contested for and became Delhi University Students Union (DUSU) president. However, there was a sense of political anticipation in the college because pitted against Ravi Gupta (the presumed candidate of the ABVP) was a tall, articulate and extremely charismatic personality who accosted me in the corridors with the words, 'Hi, I'm Arun Jaitley, and I'm contesting for college union president'. With that handshake, he earned my vote and a lifelong friendship.

It was Arun who introduced me to college debating and student politics. Come election time—and in what would be one of the biggest coups in the politics of the college—the ABVP declared Arun as their official candidate the night before the election, and he won by a landslide, having polled more than 90 per cent of the votes. If memory serves me correctly, he pulled over 900 votes to Ravi Gupta's 100 odd. The ABVP, in a bold move, stepped up to the plate and plucked from outside their ken, and thus guaranteed themselves extraordinary electoral success not only in the college union election for president but at DUSU as well in the years to come.

The next year, in 1973, when the DUSU election became a direct election—unlike the earlier years where the central counsellors, who were directly elected, voted for the DUSU candidates—Arun once again won by a landslide vote, this time, the post of DUSU vice president. Alok Kumar was elected as the DUSU president in the same election. The eagle-eyed reader will note that Alok, a lawyer by profession, is now the international working president of the Vishva Hindu Parishad (VHP). A year later, Arun once again elected by a record margin to the post of the DUSU president, and was president till

26 June 1975, when he was arrested and the union, dissolved.

This reminiscing of the college politics of the time is an important touchstone in my own journey, as it played an influential part in shaping my personal and political beliefs as well as forcing me, in many ways, to shed the introvert within me and dive head first into the sociopolitical milieu of the university. Once Arun became college president in 1972, he involved me in college and university debating (on which I will write more later) even as he enlisted me into joining the ABVP and contesting for supreme counsellor in 1973.

Of relevance to my own nascent journey and the wider political atmosphere was the bitterly fought presidential election in SRCC in 1973. The NSUI and the Congress—determined to avenge what they had considered a betrayal the year earlier by Arun—pitted Ashwini Kumar Anand against ABVP's candidate Vijay Goel, who is a dear, old friend. And though I became supreme counsellor with ABVP's support, Vijay lost in a closely fought election, leading to the NSUI defeating the ABVP on its home turf. The mantle fell on my shoulders to restore the 'status quo', as it were, in the following year. It was a four-cornered contest with Pradeep Gupta, Virendra Taneja and Azad Kumar Dhani pitted against me.

While Arun kept a watchful eye on the proceedings, the election-in-charge on behalf of the ABVP was Vijay Goel (who thirsted for revenge), and a young and exceptionally talented Hindi speaker with the promise of a great political future ahead, Rajat Sharma. The president of ABVP's Delhi unit was a professor in Swami Shraddhanand College, Prabhu Chawla, whose years of journalism were still ahead of him. The collective efforts of these stalwarts paid off. The revenge was particularly sweet, as I polled more than all the three opponents combined. Elected along with me as vice president and secretary were my close and lifelong friends Ajay Kapur and Ravi Gupta, respectively. With the ABVP also winning the DUSU election, and Arun as the president, I remember that we were able to converge student efforts to organize a first-of-its-kind college festival called Bonanza '74—a highlight of my political tenure.

The reader may wonder whether my almost-excessive name-dropping in this rumination is intended. Yes, it is! As I began writing about the politics of the time, it occurred to me that the tough and turbulent times of the 1970s not only resulted in nationwide student movements and a new stream of consciousness in Indian politics but also provided an opportunity for the abundance of talent and ambition within DU to shine and stamp their mark in the new India that was going to emerge from the chaos of the Emergency. Tough times bring out the best in people, and only the toughest survive.

The Long March

Across generations, the youth have been quick to disaffection. It was inevitable that the low years of 1973 and 1974 would result in an uprising in the educational campuses of India. Student politics at the time was taking on a national, rebellious hue—most notably the JP Andolan (formally known as the Chhatra Sangharsh Samiti, led by veteran Gandhian socialist Jayaprakash Narayan, popularly known as JP) to epitomize the large-scale disaffection that the country felt towards the rising corruption, nepotism and ill-informed policies of the government.

Bihar was where it first started, and Patna University was its birthing ground. A thin and slightly moustachioed individual, Lalu Prasad Yadav, was the university president, and his able lieutenant was a shorter and squatter individual, Ravi Shankar Prasad, who was Patna University's joint secretary at the time. Though they belonged to different political ideologies, the JP movement united them as it did almost all non-Congress organizations all over college campuses in India. The non-violent student protests that started in Bihar would soon spread to all parts of the country and find a permanent harbour in DU, before abruptly ending with the declaration of the Emergency.

JP created an All-India Student Coordination Committee and appointed Arun Jaitley as its president. Lalu Yadav and Ravi Shankar Prasad were an integral part of the committee, as was a young Arif Mohammad Khan, the president of the Aligarh Muslim University Students' Union (AMUSU). The agitations continued through 1974, and on 12 June 1975, Justice Jagmohanlal Sinha of the Allahabad High Court found PM Indira Gandhi guilty of electoral malpractice and barred her from elections for six years. She appealed to the Supreme Court with her version of events, but her real answer was given to the nation a few days later. On 25 June 1975, she declared an Emergency in the country, suspended civil liberties and jailed her opponents.

On 26 June, I woke up in Bombay at my aunt's house, where I was holidaying, and used her STD facilities to put across a call to Arun for a general 'chit-chat'. His father, Maharaj Kishen Jaitley, picked up the phone, and when I enquired about Arun, he said, '*Kaka university gaya hai* (kaka has gone to the University).' Oblivious to the news of the day, I just said '*Acha Uncle, keh dena ki mera phone tha* (Okay, Uncle, please let him know I called).' He then ventured to say, '*Suna hai India mein Emergency lagi hai* (I have heard that an Emergency has been declared).' But even then, I had no clue of what had happened. It was only at 12.30 p.m. when the afternoon papers came that things became clearer. JP, Morarji Desai, Atal Bihari Vajpayee and every other opposition leader of stature had been arrested, and so had Arun.

When I pieced the facts together later, I came to know that they had come on the night of 25 June to arrest Arun. His father, a well-known trial court lawyer, stalled them at the door while Arun escaped from behind the house, walked to his friend Kaka Bhargav's house and spent the night there. The next day, he went to the university, got a group of students together and organized what has now come to be recognized as the only 'organized protest' against the Emergency. Thereafter, Arun went to the university café for breakfast and was eating his omelette when they arrested him. It was the beginning of a 19-month incarceration.

I returned to Delhi a few days later, and after lying low for a day or two, hopped across to SRCC to survey the situation. The mood was sombre, mistrust was in the air, and everyone seemed on edge. There was a rumour that I was also on the pickup list, but there was no clarity. Two of my friends from school who were in college with me came forward offering help—the late Samir Mahajan, who was DIG Mahajan's son, said, 'Take my number down, any problem, just call me, we will get it sorted out'; the other was my friend Anil Arora, whose father was an additional district magistrate and whose uncle was Jagjivan Ram's personal assistant. Both told me not to worry, and that they would handle things if anything went wrong. I left college with them when, in the distance, we spotted a student leader with known police links. I spent a few days underground thereafter at the house of my close friend, Manu Chadha, and then when things seemed to quiet down, went back to my house.

A few days later, I learnt that the police had come looking for me at my old house in Defence Colony. On hearing this, my parents packed me off to Bombay, where I stayed for a few months, before coming back to Delhi. It was then that I reconnected with Arun in person again. We had already been exchanging letters and continued to do so throughout his stint in jail.

Arun used to be taken to court for the hearing of the Odeon Cinema case filed against him for leading the agitation outside it, which resulted in damage of property. This case—which was earlier treated like harassment—turned out to be a blessing in disguise, as it afforded us the opportunity to meet Arun. His parents, sisters and I were regular visitors, and these were outings that Arun really looked forward to. I have always marvelled at the fortitude with which Arun bore his time in jail (he was among the earliest to be arrested and the last to be released). I think, more than anything, this really forged his political outlook. In jail, as he wrote in his letters to me, he was busy reading up books on Indian history and law.

It is also important to mention that both Vijay Goel and Rajat Sharma (twice) were jailed after publicly sloganeering against the Emergency. They formed, when outside, the backbone of the student underground movement.

The warrant against me ultimately went into cold storage, and I came back to Delhi after four months. My college vice president, Ajay Kapur, was arrested as well and did a short stint in jail before being granted bail.

It is said that Mao always had a soft spot for those who joined him in the 'long march'. The Emergency had a similar effect on all those who were on its wrong side. Friendships made in those days, I have seen in retrospect, always had a greater sense of bonding.

The Best and the Brightest

In addition to friendships forged during the Emergency, I find myself thinking about the time spent debating. It is no stretch at all to say that debating was, by far, the most popular extracurricular activity in the university back then.

I myself am a by-product of two universities, having studied first in Delhi and then in Bombay, and was lucky to have participated in debating in both cities. After Arun left, I captained the SRCC team in Delhi, and a few years later, captained Government Law College (GLC) in Bombay. I can, therefore, say with some authority that DU and its debaters could hold their own against any other university—and this can proudly be claimed even today.

The campus, particularly, was filled with debating opportunity, and colleges like St. Stephen's, Hindu, Miranda House, Indraprastha College, SRCC and Law Faculty, all hosted several intra- and inter-college debates every year, which not only brought forward the best debating talent but also a substantial audience. The smaller debates would pull 150-odd people, while the big debates saw over 400 people in the audience. We also had a few 'all-India competitions', which brought talent from all over, including, most notably, St. Xavier's, Calcutta, and the various IITs.

Part of the popularity, I believe, was the prizes. The winning team in a big debate would take home the trophy, but each of the individual winners got a neat amount of cash by way of an individual prize. Winning, therefore, gave you splurging rights—at a time when the whopping 'Submarine Sandwich' at the Parlour in Connaught Place cost six bucks, a hundred rupees by way of a cash prize went a long way in supplementing your spending money.

The fun in debating was compounded by the audience's participation. Not only did they come in large numbers to cheer their teams but they also participated by interjecting at the end of each debate with questions to the concerned speaker. Shahid Amin (Professor Amin) was a legendary interjector, much feared for his incisive dissection of one's speech. There was also this tradition of throwing the debate 'open' to the house, where members of the audience would also speak. From Hindu College, my friend Anoop Bose (a lawyer today) would often address us from both sides of the floor.

The fierce rivalry was between St. Stephen's and Hindu, and the two most prestigious debates—the Mukarji Memorial and the CF Andrews Trophy—were both held at St. Stephen's. In my first year, Arun and I represented SRCC and won the Andrews. Arun came first, me fourth, and we were up against the debaters who came second and third. We won because the distance between Arun and the person coming in second was more than the distance between the person who came third and me.

One of the best ways to highlight the talent at play would be to enumerate the debaters of that era, and where they went on to in later life. When you see where these people ended up, you understand their extraordinary calibre. From SRCC, there was Arun and me, and I was later joined by Rohinton Nariman and Navtej Sarna. Arun, as we all know, became one of the country's top lawyers, joining politics later on and ended his political career as the finance and defence minister of India. Rohinton, after his career as one of the country's top lawyers, was directly appointed a judge of the Supreme Court and became one of the better judges of his time. Sarna was our ambassador to Israel and the US, and high commissioner to the UK.

Debating against me and Arun from Hindu College was the prime minister of the college parliament Hardeep Singh Puri. Ambassador Puri, as he is known today, became a career diplomat, becoming the president of the United Nations Security Council in 2011, and today is a senior minister in the Narendra Modi Cabinet, serving as the minister of petroleum and natural gas, and minister of housing and urban affairs. Seconding him from Hindu College was Suresh Kumar, who left India and became assistant commerce secretary for trade promotion in 2010 in the Barack Obama administration.

Stephen's, of course, had a brilliant debating team that comprised Shashi Tharoor, Ramu Damodaran and Arun Singh. Adding to the fire power was a young Swapan Dasgupta. Shashi was not only a minister of the Union Cabinet in the UPA regime between 2009 and 2014, he was also the under-secretary-general of the United Nations (UN), and in 2006, contested for the post of the secretary general. Ambassador Damodaran today works in the UN and served as the executive assistant to PM Narasimha Rao from 1991 to 1994. Arun Singh, the third limb of the team, served as ambassador to the US. Swapan became a well-known journalist and was the president's nominee to the Rajya Sabha.

The Faculty of Law, in those days, was represented by Pavan Varma, again an erstwhile ambassador and Member of Parliament. There were many other debaters, most of whom

I have not mentioned for the paucity of space, but I hope that the quality of the names mentioned above bear witness to the fact that DU of the time was home to the best and brightest minds.

Most people, when they reminisce about old times, often feel that the time they had was the best and the most momentous. I am no different. I leave it to the readers to judge if they agree with me.

AN ISLAND CALLED D-SCHOOL

Bibek Debroy

I studied in the Delhi School of Economics (DSE) or D-School, as it is often called, from 1974 to 1976. I did my master's in economics from there. At the time, when people less enlightened would sometimes ask me where I studied, on hearing D-School, they would cast a sceptical glance towards me. Wasn't I a bit too old to be studying in a school? In India, American nomenclature isn't as common as the British.

D-School was, and is, part of Delhi University. It is the postgraduate department for economics, commerce, sociology and geography. It is geographically located in North Campus, Maurice Nagar, named after Sir Maurice Linford Gwyer, who was the vice chancellor of DU from 1938 to 1950. Yet, DSE—particularly, the economics department—conveyed an impression of being an island, 'entire of itself'. To continue with John Donne, it was of course 'a piece of the continent, a part of the main' that was DU.

The trigger for this anthology is the university's centennial celebrations in 2022. Modern universities were set up towards

Hardeep S. Puri, Prime-Minister (seated fourth from left), *with cabinet ministers of the Hindu College Parliament, 1970–71*

Courtesy: Hardeep S. Puri

Sanjeev Sanyal (standing extreme left) *poses with his classmates from Shri Ram College of Commerce in a University Special bus, 1991*

Courtesy: Sanjeev Sanyal

His Holiness the 14th Dalai Lama plants a sapling during his visit to Lady Shri Ram College, 1992

Courtesy: Meenkshi Gopinath

Shashi Tharoor (standing, top right, dressed in white) *reacts after winning the St. Stephen's College students' union presidency, 1974*
Courtesy: Shashi Tharoor

Meenakshi Gopinath welcoming distinguished alumna Aung San Suu Kyi during the latter's visit to Lady Shri Ram College, 2012. Also seen in the background is Shashi Tharoor
Courtesy: Meenakshi Gopinath

At the vanguard of history as a discipline: Faculty of Arts building
Courtesy: Office of Hardeep S. Puri

The power centre steeped in history and culture: Vice Chancellor's office, formerly Viceregal Lodge
Courtesy: Office of Hardeep S. Puri

Lakshmi Puri (left) *poses with Manju Jain soon after graduation from Lady Shri Ram College, 1973*
Courtesy: Lakshmi Puri

Imtiaz Ali (right) *with his friend Sujeet Jha in Hindu College premises, 1992*
Courtesy: Imtiaz Ali

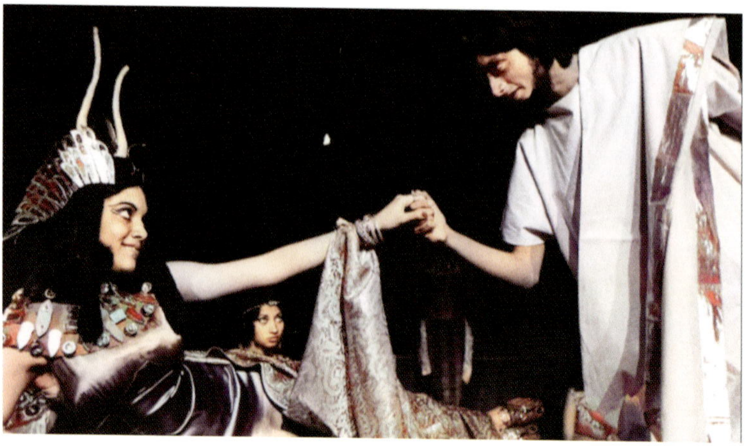

Shashi Tharoor and Mira Nair star in St. Stephen's College Shakespeare Society production of Antony and Cleopatra, *1974*
Courtesy: Shashi Tharoor

Kiren Rijiju (second from right) *with students and faculty of the Delhi Law School, 1992*
Courtesy: Kiren Rijiju

Arnab Goswami (seated left) *is seen with Imtiaz Ali* (seated right) *with other friends at Hindu College, 1992*
Courtesy: Arnab Goswami

Meenakshi Gopinath presents a memento to Vice Chancellor Dinesh Singh, 2013
Courtesy: Meenakshi Gopinath

Entry into a pan-India institution: one of the gates of DU's North Campus
Courtesy: Office of Hardeep S. Puri

Open-air theatre at Hindu College: carving a niche in the university theatre circuit
Courtesy: Office of Hardeep S. Puri

the middle of the nineteenth century—Calcutta, Madras and Bombay being the first, in 1857. Delhi was a late entrant. In 1882, a commission was set up to examine the educational system, commonly known as the Hunter Commission. This said, 'The function of these Universities is that of examination, and not of instruction. The latter is conducted by the affiliated colleges and other institutions authorised to send up candidates for the university examinations.'[1] This decentralized system was modelled on systems then prevalent in Britain. Universities subsequently started to teach, but that unitary versus affiliating dichotomy remained.

This doesn't mean there weren't colleges in Delhi. The earliest was in 1792, a private college. To quote from the Hunter Commission, 'In 1792, an Oriental College, supported by voluntary contributions from Muhammadan gentlemen, was founded at Delhi for the study of Persian and Arabic, but owing to the reduced circumstances of the patrons the funds failed.'[2] Plus, there was the public Delhi College, of 1825 vintage. 'In 1825, a Government college was opened at Delhi under the Committee of Public Instruction; and in 1829, it was endowed by a munificent bequest of Rs. 1,70,000 from the Nawab Itimad-ud-Daula, Prime Minister

---

[1]Debroy, Bibek, 'Education policy: The exit of affiliation', *The New Indian Express*, 9 August 2020, https://bit.ly/3wh0APh. Accessed on 2 May 2022.
[2]Goverment of India, Report of The Indian Education Commission, Superintendent of Goverment Printing, Calcutta, 1883, https://bit.ly/3vQ6hDe. Accessed on 2 May 2022.

of the King of Oudh.'[3]

There were changes after 1857. Administratively, Delhi moved from the North-Western Provinces to Punjab. The Delhi College went through various stages of closing, reopening and fresh closure. The 1907 version of *Imperial Gazetteer* states, 'The principal educational institution was, until 1877, the Delhi College, founded in 1792, but abolished in 1877, in order to concentrate higher education in the Punjab University at Lahore.'[4] Today's Zakir Husain Delhi College traces its antecedents to both the Oriental and Delhi colleges. St. Stephen's College was established in 1881, Hindu College in 1899 and Ramjas College in 1917. I mention these three in particular because these were the three colleges that established DU, in a way. DSE came much later. Before DSE, it wasn't the case that economics wasn't taught. DU's 'Calendar' for 1922–23 gives us a list of faculty members who taught economics. They were from St. Stephen's, Hindu and Ramjas.

Those early universities were under the affiliating system and had wide territorial jurisdiction. The National Education Policy (NEP) 2020 has views on the affiliating system. Among the problems ailing higher education, it lists 'large affiliating universities resulting in low standards of undergraduate education.'[5] But that change in the character of institutions

---

[3]Ibid.

[4]Cotton, James Sutherland, Sir Richard Burn and Sir William Stevenson Meyer, *Imperial Gazetteer of India*, Great Britain, Clarendon Press, 1907.

[5]Debroy, Bibek, 'Education policy: The exit of affiliation', *The New Indian Express*, 9 August 2020, https://bit.ly/3wh0APh. Accessed on 2 May 2022.

of higher education is in the future. In the present, DU is an affiliating university, with more than 75 affiliating colleges, centres, institutions and faculties that straddle an array of disciplines.

In 1922, there were four affiliating colleges—St. Stephen's, Hindu, Ramjas and Delhi College. The background was the Sadler University Commission (1917–19). Though dubbed a University Commission, it was actually a commission set up to study the functioning of the Calcutta University (CU). Since the first lot of universities didn't teach and only examined, the Sadler Commission recommended a transition to unitary teaching and residential universities.

Meanwhile, thc capital moved from Calcutta to Delhi. DU's Calendar for 1922–23 explains this transition for us:

> Following this recommendation, the Universities of Allahabad and the Panjab commenced to consider re-shaping their constitution, and as the Delhi Colleges were then affiliated to the University of the Panjab while some of their students went to Allahabad to prosecute their studies in post-graduate courses, the Government of India felt the necessity of providing an independent University for the students of its Capital City. The Delhi University Act was the result. It was brought into force from the 1st May, 1922, by a Notification published in the Gazette of India, dated 11th March, 1922.[6]

Today, DU's emblem has the expression 'निष्ठा धृतिः सत्यम्',

[6]The University of Delhi, Calendar 1922–23.

conceptualized by Lachhmi Dhar Kalla, the former head of the Department of Oriental Languages. But in 1922, the logo of the elephant, the book, the lotuses and the Yamuna flowing at the back didn't exist. Instead, the expression was 'Scientia et Mores', and the images were completely different.

It wasn't smooth sailing initially. Government finances were under pressure, and the university's grant was slashed from the initial Rs. 75,000 to Rs. 40,000. More importantly, there was the Indian Retrenchment Committee 1922–23, known as the Inchcape Committee, which suggested financial conditions did not warrant the start of a new university. But since DU had already been set up, there was no question of rolling anything back. From that first calendar, I find that on 7 June 1922, K.C. Nag, from St. Stephen's College, was appointed as 'Reader' for a period of two years.

Yarrow Visited

I did my BA in economics from Presidency College, Calcutta, now Presidency University (with economics becoming increasingly mathematical, the course is now called BSc. At that time, it was BA). As a student and as a teacher, in part of my subsequent career, I am convinced that the hallmark of good teaching in economics is rigour in the teaching of economic theory (broadly divided into microeconomics and macroeconomics) and statistics/econometrics. With those skills, everything else can be learnt and can be self-taught. In those days, from 1970 to 1973, Presidency College possessed the best undergraduate teaching faculty (for economic theory) in the country, though that wasn't true of statistics/econometrics. This was despite the political turmoil in West Bengal then. Most students who pursued a master's degree in economics did so at the postgraduate department of CU. A handful (four or five) followed the movement to the capital and turned up in Delhi. The human capital flight to Jawaharlal Nehru University (JNU) hadn't quite started. Delhi meant DSE. For some unclear reason, this movement to Delhi usually occurred in alternate years, not every year. Two years before us, there were Ashok Lahiri, Amal Sanyal and Bhaskar Dutta. Two years after us, there were Dilip Mukherjee, Omkar Goswami and Dilip Cherian.

I would probably have turned up in D-School in any case. But some advice aided the decision. Ashok Mitra was the chief economic adviser (CEA) from 1970 to 1972. My father worked in Calcutta at the time and he knew Mitra professionally. Amartya Sen was passing through the city and was a guest in Mitra's house for a few days. Using his acquaintance with Mitra, my father fixed up an appointment for his callow son to meet Amartya Sen. Given my age, there was a single-point agenda for that conversation, which lasted a bare few minutes. Should I study for my master's in Calcutta or should I explore DSE? I remember the response. 'I have left. Pranab [Bardhan] isn't there. [He was probably away in Berkeley at the time.] Sukhamoy [Chakraborty] doesn't teach any more. [He was with the Planning Commission and was on leave.] Arjun [Sengupta] isn't there. [He joined the government.] Manmohan [Singh] has left. That's no great loss. [He became CEA.] But I still think you should join DSE.' That remark about Dr Manmohan Singh was somewhat uncharitable, I thought. Unlike the other names mentioned, Dr Singh may not have done much research. However, his students (those who studied international trade) have told me he was a wonderful teacher.

Thus, four of us from Presidency College then trundled off to Delhi. While the admission process was going on, I stayed with a friend of my father's in Chittaranjan Park, which was called EPDP (East Pakistan Displaced Persons) Colony then. It was still sparsely populated and not that well-connected. Admission to D-School involved taking a written test, unless you happened to have done your undergraduate degree in economics from DU and had received a first class. The question paper for the admission test was remarkable, testing the student's ingenuity (later, we were told it had been set by Prasanta Pattanaik).

After years, memory cannot be trusted, especially on numbers. I recall that only 65 students could be admitted into DSE proper. However, DSE was also DU's postgraduate department for teaching economics. Therefore, the total class strength was 150. The others also studied for MA, but were enrolled through a college, not D-School.

Depending on what destiny decided for you, there were two differences. First, classes were common, but there were special DSE tutorials for those enrolled through D-School, and those were exceptionally good. Those enrolled through colleges presumably had tutorials in their respective colleges, and perhaps those weren't that good. Second, there was the question of a hostel. Colleges had their own hostels, and admission into one of these was more or less certain. For those registering through DSE, there was Gwyer Hall and a postgraduate hostel for women. Admission was on the basis of marks. Scoring high marks in CU was difficult, relative to DU, and there was no written admission test for hostels. For any educational institution, a hosteller's perspective will always be different from that of a day scholar. In terms of experiencing university life, the former will be fuller, though DTC's University Special buses also had a life of their own. In the initial months, I stayed as a paying guest. Subsequently, my father got transferred to Delhi.

DSE's alumni list is impressive and its faculty, illustrious. I have in mind economics, though this is also true of the other D-School departments, as it is true of DU in general. There are reasons why DU does so well in university rankings, including cross-country ones. When we walked in as students, we were of course not aware of the legacy of DSE, set up in 1949 by a great institution builder V.K.R.V. Rao. As we walked into the hallowed precincts of the college, it seemed odd that the entry was through a side gate, located on what is now Sudhir Bose Marg (at that time, it was called Imperial Avenue, but I don't remember anyone referring to it by that name). The main gate was on Prof ND Kapoor Marg, diagonally opposite Kirori Mal College. As long as we were students, we never saw that main gate open. The urban legend was that it would be thrown open when someone associated with D-School won the Nobel Memorial Prize in Economic Sciences. I have heard a rumour that there was an attempt to open the main gate when Amartya Sen visited, after winning the prize, but the gate fell down. This may very well be canard.

Whenever I have visited an alma mater after years, the visit has been reminiscent of Wordsworth's 'Yarrow Visited'. This wasn't quite what my fancy cherished. I am referring to the physical size of the building, nothing more. As a student, it seems to be huge, imposing and gigantic. As you grow and are exposed to more impressive structures, the revisited building seems to be relatively small, compared to what you imagined it to be.

This was particularly so when after several years Mrinal Datta Chaudhuri or MDC, as he was commonly known, invited me to the department to deliver a talk on law and economics. The building, Ratan Tata Library, the canteen where we spent hours, the café in the adjacent Faculty of Management Studies—all seemed smaller than what my memory retained. But I must admit that the vice chancellor's office and VC Lawns were an exception to this principle, perhaps because those were out of bounds while we were students. In 2019, the then vice chancellor, Yogesh Tyagi, invited me to deliver a talk for Percipience—the Eminent Alumni Lecture Series. The grounds—blooming with flowers in February—were spectacular and magnificent.

Once admitted to the DSE, there was a separate interview for a scholarship, funded by the University Grants Commission

(UGC). On the interview board was S.P. Nag, a faculty member who taught industrial economics. Though I am not certain if he was related to the legendary K.C. Nag, his name rarely features in the list of illustrious DSE faculty. At least, illustrious alumni rarely mention him. Nag asked me the first question, which, as it turned out, became the only question. Here is the question, almost in his words: 'Manmohan Singh went on a visit to USA. Being somewhat absent-minded, he forgot to carry any money with him. However, he was well-known in USA. For his board and lodging and for everything else, wherever he went, he paid by issuing IOUs and signing them. He was so well-known that these IOUs were accepted everywhere. He thought, once back in India, he would honour these IOUs by remitting the money owed. However, being absent-minded, he forgot. Who paid for Manmohan Singh's stay in USA?' I have no idea why Nag chose Manmohan Singh as a name. He wasn't that famous then. Perhaps because Manmohan Singh was a colleague who had recently left. Perhaps because Manmohan Singh was the CEA, and he thought I would recognize the name.

No special intelligence was needed on my part to answer the question, courtesy the teaching I received in Presidency from Mihir Rakshit, one of the best teachers of macroeconomics in the country then (the other one, S.B. Gupta, taught us in DSE). Without having to think, I replied, 'Money supply went up. Prices increased. Everyone in USA paid.' I got my scholarship on the basis of that single question.

Every educational institution goes through ups and

downs. The hallmark of a good educational institution is that the quality of teaching never drops below a threshold. Amartya Sen was right; some noted teachers had left, including Jagdish Bhagwati, whose name Amartya Sen did not mention. However, we did have exceptional teachers. Given my jaundiced view, my bias is towards economic theory and statistics/econometrics. For microeconomics, there was Prasanta Pattanaik. For macroeconomics, there was S.B. Gupta. For statistics/econometrics, there were A.L. Nagar, K.L. Krishna and Balbir Singh (who later died in the 1985 Air India Kanishka bombing).

The other teachers didn't leave much of a mark. Perhaps I was simply not interested in those other courses, except for the one on Indian economic policy. The courses today are, of course, different from what they used to be then. At the time, why were we asked to study economic history of Britain, Japan, United States and the Soviet Union? (In fairness, this was standard fare in many similar courses elsewhere in India.)

In our time, DSE had become abstract and esoteric, somewhat delinked from reality. Unlike the 1950s and 1960s, when D-School faculty were part of policy debates and contributed to them, in our time, DSE had lost some of its relevance in impacting India's economic policymaking. For Indian economic policy, we were required to mug up plan models. The Second Five Year Plan (1951–56) model was part for the course and the rationale behind the model was obvious and necessary. But, while we were students, the rage was the Fourth Five Year Plan (1969–74) model, a consistency model. The reasoning was never made clear. Nevertheless, in the examination, we were expected to reproduce equations of that 30-sector model.

Today's course structure is different. In our time, there were 16 courses, each accounting for 50 marks. The examination was divided into two parts, Part-I and Part-II, each of 400 marks. Part-I came at the end of the first year and you were examined on eight courses, all compulsory, that is, core. There were no options. Two were on economic theory (micro and macro), two on statistics, one on Indian economic history, one on post-Independence economic development in India and one on that frustrating economic history of other countries. Then the eighth course was probably some version of essential mathematics.

Part-II came at the end of the second year, and two of the eight courses were compulsory, probably advanced versions of micro and macro. The remaining six were electives, and you could choose from a basket. I chose advanced economic theory (two courses), economics of socialism (two courses) and econometrics (two courses). As students, we called econometrics 'Tricks'. Once I chose advanced economic theory, I was also taught by MDC, a great teacher, who was appreciated much more in one-on-one or small group interactions rather than in a class with a size of 150. I also remember Raj Krishna, who took a few lectures, though he was technically employed in the Agricultural Economics Research Centre (AERC).

The 150 students were a mixed bag, with diverse

backgrounds, and seemed to be connected with the Pareto principle or the 80/20 rule. To take Pareto's original example, 80 per cent of the land will be owned by 20 per cent of the population. However, this principle seems to work in alumni groups. From several interactions, I know—directly or indirectly—about what has happened to 20 per cent of my fellow students. The remaining 80 per cent have vanished. That's also true of classmates from school or Presidency. In our class, few remained in academia proper. Ajay Chhibber and Santosh Panda are probably the only others. Uday Sekhar started off as one but branched off. There are some who became teachers in various colleges. There are several in the civil services, now retired, including Pradeep Kumar Sinha, formerly Cabinet Secretary and principal advisor to PM Narendra Modi.

For those joining the civil services, it was common practice to take up a job (if you did sufficiently well in your MA exam) as lecturer in one of the DU colleges, while you prepared for the Union Public Service Commission (UPSC) exam. I had no intention of sitting for the civil service examinations. In the final year of master's, I got a scholarship to go to Trinity College, Cambridge. Consequently, my father gave up his attempt of badgering me about UPSC. Before leaving for Cambridge, I had a lecturer's job in Kirori Mal College, at a basic pay of ₹700 per month. That was my first job and yet another association with DU.

Those 150 students divided themselves up into various close-knit groups. Those were the comfort zones. For a start,

DSE students were snooty about non-DSE ones. Those with undergraduate degrees from St. Stephen's were snooty about everyone else and hung around together. To make matters worse, there was rivalry between the St. Stephen's crowd and the limited few from Presidency. Inevitably, other than Presidency classmates, my closest friends became others who came from outside Delhi (such as Odisha), Bengalis from Delhi (irrespective of which college they had studied in) and those from Hansraj, Kirori Mal and Hindu. It changed subsequently.

I am reasonably certain D-School has no notion of a 'record' for marks scored in the MA exam. But it was urban legend that there was such a record and that it was held by Pankaj Tandon, who had scored 608/800 (it was easier to score such marks if all six of your electives were 'Tricks', instead of two). It was also urban legend that Rahul Khullar (two years before me) had tried to break it and had scored 603/800. When we joined as students, Rahul was a bit of a cult figure. Later, I got to know him (and his wife Sindhushree) very well but never bothered to ask him whether that legend was true. One year before me, Dinkar Khullar tried to break the record and scored 598/800. Hence, a story circulated that I was going to have a shot at it as well. I have no idea how you try to break a record in an examination apart from doing the best you can. I topped the Part-I exam, and Uday Sekhar (from St. Stephen's) was second, a considerable distance away.

Friends who thrived on that rivalry between Presidency and St. Stephen's reported that the real threat wasn't Uday Sekhar but Arjun Ray (also from St. Stephen's). DSE had a system that if you didn't do as well as you expected in your Part-I examination, you could take a repeat examination, along with your Part-II exam. However, if you ventured to do that, the second set of marks would hold, not the better of the two. Arjun, who hadn't done that badly in Part-I, decided to repeat all eight Part-I courses. Having performed much better, I, too, decided to repeat my two statistics courses. Classmates passed remarks about these two mad Bengalis.

As it happened, I ended up getting one mark less in statistics and Arjun also lost marks in statistics, though he gained in the other courses. I ended with 593/600. I was thus awarded the K.C. Nag Memorial Economics Prize (a set of books) and the Hiralal Bhargava gold medal, as every D-School topper does every year. K.C. Nag is understandable. But I wonder how many of those toppers know who Hiralal Bhargava, the famous calligrapher, poet and printer, actually was. I recommend his travelogue and semi-biographical account of calligraphy be included in the set of books awarded as prizes.

My scholarship in Trinity was on the basis of my Part-I marks. When I submitted my final marks, there was one mark less in Part-I, and I received a telegram (those were the days) from my senior tutor in Trinity, asking for an explanation for this peculiar phenomenon. With six 'Tricks', Dilip Mukherjee reportedly broke the record two years later.

I have conveyed the impression that DSE was an island, irrespective of the political turmoil all around us. It was that, an island, even during the Emergency. Of course, that island syndrome was compounded by my being a day scholar. Delhi University Students' Union (DUSU) elections became events (Arun Jaitley was the president) and there were protests, censorship and imprisonment. By and large, this didn't touch D-School. It wasn't the Law Faculty and was slightly delinked from reality. Yes, there were non-political debates, college festivals and the annual cricket match (typically, a Hindu versus St. Stephen's final).

Two years of my life. I learnt some economics. I made some friends. D-School was a launch pad to go abroad. At a personal level, I became part of that human capital flight from Calcutta to Delhi. Amartya Sen was right. In opting for D-School and DU over CU, I made a wise decision. In 1974, I hadn't read the Sadler Commission's report. But wasn't that what Sadler had essentially said? The capital had moved. Therefore, Delhi should become the centre of intellectual pursuits. In a hundred years, DU has become the core and trigger for exactly that.

HERVOICE@DU.100: ENGENDERING THE ACADEMY

Meenakshi Gopinath

Centenaries generate expectations. Centennials, socialized into the World Wide Web, assert myriad claims. Between these impulses, as Delhi University navigates its own 'pluriverse of aspiration' in this hundredth year of existence, its sheer diversity, scale, reputation and history signal the salience of the public university in India today.

With the growing focus internationally on learning as a public, non-commodified good, 'Socially Responsible Higher Education'[1] finds resonance today. The idea of the university as 'Ivory Tower' has been replaced by that of the 'engaged' university expected to link 'town' and 'gown'. It invokes a commitment to a knowledge democracy and to epistemic justice, including the decolonization of the mind and the breaking down of hierarchies between disciplines and knowledge systems. Embedded in this is the vision of

[1]Hall, Budd, and Rajesh Tandon (eds), *Socially Responsible Higher Education: International Perspectives on Knowledge Democracy*, Brill Sense, Leiden/Boston, 2021.

a space where diverse disciplines can be on offer, as also diverse methodologies where students and faculty from diverse regions, social groups and backgrounds find opportunities for nurture, discovery and growth, and where multiple intelligences can thrive. This imagination foregrounds not only academic nurture but also dialogic, ruminative, creative, democratic, collaborative and inclusive spaces, which transcend conventional borders and boundaries—both geographic and conceptual. Today, the academy is charged with the additional mandate of engendering its ethos.

The unprecedented growth in the enrolment of women in higher education institutes (HEIs) in India and the constitutional provision for equality makes this all the more compelling. An apposite conceptual lexicon, finding utterance now, strives for acceptance, visibility and resonance within DU. Public universities are not merely transactional hubs of teaching and learning. They are social institutions that animate a new reality and establish the terms of civilized engagement in democratic citizenship.

A 'microcosm of the Republic of India' is how the DU is often described.[2] In terms of its size, heterogeneity, location, its noisy yet vibrant 'democracy-in-the-making' rhythms, it is a central university like no other. The pulse of this complex variegated space—that has on its rolls more than 6,06,228 students from different parts of the country—is most felt in its colleges. The bulk of its students and faculty identify

[2]The analogy is attributed to Prof. Deepak Nayyar, vice chancellor of Delhi University between 2000 and 2005.

primarily with their colleges, and through them, vicariously, with the university. As in the rest of India, where nearly 80 per cent of the total student population are undergraduate, the majority of DU's demographic dividend resides in its colleges—2,11,590 undergraduate to 29,651 postgraduate students (2020-21).[3]

Primarily a 'collegiate' university, with 16 faculties and 86 departments today, DU has 77 constituent (of 91 affiliated) colleges spread across its North and South campuses. Of these, the 22 women's colleges (constituting 28.57 per cent) have played a significant role in engendering the DU ethos. They collectively provide a fecund ecosystem for the impulse of inclusivity, diversity, intersectionality and equality within the academy, even as their trajectories have been varied and uneven.

Sir Maurice Gwyer, the fifth vice chancellor (1938–50), who is frequently invoked in this anthology, was the 'visionary extraordinaire' of DU. He wished to fashion the university as 'worthy of the capital city of India reflecting in its "intellect and culture" the destiny of the Indian people'[4], to which teachers and students would come from afar, and whose degrees would

---

[3]Additionally, 3,26,830 students were enrolled in the distance education mode and 32,209 non-collegiate women students also form part of this mammoth university. The total enrolment across conventional and distance mode in all programmes was 6,06,228 in 2020–21. See: *University of Delhi: Highlights 2021*, p.4, https://tinyurl.com/2d3ykfp5. Accessed on 24 May 2022

[4]Aparna Basu cited in Hasan, Mushirul (ed.), *Knowledge, Power and Politics: Educational Institutions in India*, Roli Books, New Delhi, 1998, p. 84.

be a mark of distinction wherever 'learning and culture are held in veneration'.[5]

With political and administrative power along with commercial interests gravitating to Delhi in the 1920s, and the sweeping demographic and cultural alterations to the fabric of its social structure from then on, through Partition and after, profound changes became visible in the ethos of the pioneer colleges. As Delhi grew into a metropolis, with more students from affluent 'official' families, career preferences markedly shifted towards joining the bureaucracy. Into this space of elite, mostly male privilege, came a new entrant in 1924. The Indraprastha College for Women (IP College) not only provided a unique niche for women to access higher education of quality, it substantially changed the terms of engagement on 'inclusion'. The attempts to 'engender' the university can be traced back to the spirited pioneers of IP College.

Framing a Palimpsest

While academic enrichment provided the basic minimum of its endeavour, IP College nurtured women to be engaged citizens—as the 'subjects', not objects, of history. From their spirited participation in the freedom movement to the post-Partition rehabilitation efforts for refugees or their involvement from the late 1960s and 1970s in protests for equal pay, dignity and against gender-based violence, IP

[5]Sir Maurice Gwyer cited in Ibid. 85.

College provided a valuable palimpsest on which newer women's colleges of DU scripted their own activism. They began to breach bastions of patriarchy well before the formal vocabulary of 'feminism' had found resonance.

With the establishment of Lady Irwin College in 1932 and the fulfilment of Gwyer's cherished project, Miranda House, in 1948, women's colleges of DU had made inroads into the coveted space of science education. After Independence, Miranda House replaced the Kinnaird College for Women (KCW), Lahore, as the place where 'emancipated' and progressive women found nurturance. It set itself a little apart from the more homespun (Khadi) preferences of IP College with an exclusive 'blue stocking' image.

Yet, together as illustrious foremothers, they set benchmarks for generations of women entering the higher education space at DU. As Andre Beteille has pointed out, in India, the university and the college have played a more significant part in the social emancipation of women than any public institution. And whereas it took Cambridge and Oxford several centuries to open their doors to women, DU was ready to graduate women within a few years of its opening.[6]

Along with IP College and Lady Irwin, women's colleges starting from the venerable Bethune College (1879) in Calcutta to Queen Mary's (1914) in Madras Presidency, SNDT Women's University (1916) in Bombay, Kanya Maha Vidyalaya (KMV) in Jalandhar (with antecedents that go as

---

[6]Beteille, Andre, 'Universities as Public Institutions', *Higher Education in India,* Jandhyala B.G Tilak (ed.), Orient BlackSwan, 2013, p. 531.

far back as 1890) were crucibles of change and opportunity for women in the pre-Independence period. Although the nationalist movement, spurred by Gandhi, brought an unprecedented number of women into the public sphere, their right to education largely remained couched within the discourse of making 'better homes, better families and better society'.[7] The 'emancipation' of women was perceived largely as the concern of progressive and reformist men.

The names of several pioneering women who blazed an impressive trail in national and international forums—beginning with the 15 women members of our Constituent Assembly—are seldom invoked. These include a Dalit woman (Dakshayani Velayudhan), a Muslim (Begum Aizaz Rasul), a Christian (Annie Mascarene), a Sikh (Rajkumari Amrit Kaur) and also Hansa Mehta, who was able to rescript the United Nation's Universal Declaration of Human Rights (UDHR) to include all human beings and not just men. Despite their sterling championing efforts, their contributions remained almost invisible in official discourse.

These biases were to be hotly contested and interrogated in the discourse that gathered momentum in several of the

---

[7]Prime Minister Jawaharlal Nehru's comments in 1950 at a women's college of DU that 'women being chiefly responsible' for running the home, would be enabled by education to do this in 'an orderly and aesthetic way', reflected the 'liberal' opinion of the time. See Banerjee, Nirmala, 'Whatever Happened to the Dreams of Modernity: The Nehruvian Era and Women's Position', *Economic & Political Weekly,* vol. 33, no. 17, 1998, pp. WS2–WS7, https://bit.ly/3L9b1um. Accessed on 22 April 2022.

women's colleges of DU from the late 1970s onward. The impact of the autonomous women's movements and women's activism became visible. The seeds sown at IP College and Miranda House had developed shoots much beyond their hallowed precincts. With the iconic *Towards Equality* report of the Committee on the Status of Women in India in 1974 came the dramatic turning point in the discourse on women's education in India. It also provided the fillip for women's studies and the setting up of women's development cells (WDCs) in the academy. Women's colleges of DU, like Lady Shri Ram College (LSR), were among the first to establish WDCs.

Expanding Horizons

Responding to the growing need for the education of women, industrialist and philanthropist Sir Shri Ram laid the foundations of LSR in 1956 in memory of his wife. An educationist at heart, he was known to fiercely guard the independence of colleges from 'interference' by government and even the university. He brought a formidable track record as chairman, board member and benefactor of three other colleges, including IP College. His vision for LSR as its founder-chairman was to provide a space where women could thrive unfettered and explore intellectual, creative and professional aspirations. This was the space that I was privileged to inhabit for nearly five decades—first as student, then as teacher and consequently as principal.

With remarkable foresight, Sir Shri Ram anticipated the

growth trajectory of Delhi as moving south. And so, it was in 1958 that the college moved from its modest beginnings in a school building in Daryaganj to a spacious campus bordering what is today Kailash Colony in South Delhi. LSR became a major landmark on the map of the relentlessly expanding city in the 1960s and early 1970s. His choice of location, in all probability, stemmed from a vision to secure enough land to expand into a future university of excellence akin to SNDT.[8]

The college building, in the late Indo-Deco style of the 1950s, represents historically the first stage of the expansion of DU from its original epicentre in the north to meet the city's burgeoning demand for access to higher education of quality for women. The building symbolizes the metaphor of women stepping out to prepare themselves for the rigours and challenges of a then newly independent nation. The cloistered red-brick courtyards and arches of the 1930s and 1940s gave way to a new architectural vocabulary of verandas and columns opening, both vertically and horizontally, to the winds of change.[9]

The provision of expansive landscapes for learning continues to animate the collective consciousness of the college. Learning,

---

[8]Another location on offer, closer to the centre of the city was a smaller plot in Lodhi Road. But Lala Shri Ram's choice was activated by a more futuristic vision. To ensure that the distance was not a deterrent, he even arranged to bus students and faculty to the new campus.

[9]From its modest beginnings with 11 faculty, 13 support staff, 243 students and seven subjects of study, LSR today sits on a 15-acre campus, with over 3,000 students, 150 faculty, 60 support staff and 15 full-fledged departments, both undergraduate and postgraduate.

not confined merely to the classroom or received curricula, is embellished by a rich co-curricular engagement that pushes the envelope of creativity in theatre, debate, music, art and a whole range of outreach initiatives. Artists, poets, writers and cultural icons spent months as 'Visiting Scholars in Residence' interacting with students and faculty to enrich the repertoire of creative engagement.[10] From the early 1990s, its 'five pillars of conscientisation'[11] channelled the focus on democratic participation in the belief that women must take the lead in scripting the new social compact for a more inclusive world.

In addition to outreach for the marginalized and underserved communities, especially during natural disasters, students stood against the tide of domineering populism while joining forces with progressive initiatives during the anti-Sikh riots of 1984; resisting the atavistic impulses of the anti-Mandal agitation that had engulfed DU; the destruction of the Babri Masjid in 1992 and so on. They threw in their lot with the feminist mobilization around the infamous Roop

---

[10]Interest in the parallel cinema movement led to the formation of the Film Club PROJEKT in 1977. It became the first collegiate society in DU to be affiliated with the prestigious Federation of Film Societies in India (FFSI). In 1987 alone, more than 50 films, from all over the world, were screened, and several renowned personalities of the 'New Wave' visited, lectured and even premiered a few films at LSR.

[11]ABHAYA (the renamed women's development cell); VAPP (the Voluntary Agency Placement Program); DHYANA (the Society for Awareness and Mindfulness); REACH (Reaffirming Equity, Access, Capacity and Humanism) and SWAVLAMBAN (the Equal Opportunities Cell) propelled this vision.

Kanwar sati case; the Vishakha case; the Nirbhaya case and the march to Raisina Hill, among others, in calling out intolerance, violence and misogyny.[12] The college was equally enthusiastic in celebrating the collapse of the Berlin Wall, and the end of Apartheid and the release of Nelson Mandela as well as mobilizing support through its Human Rights Forum for the release of its illustrious alumna, Aung San Suu Kyi.

The institutionalization of transparent procedures of admission, through a much sought-after parallel extracurricular activities track, was first formalized at LSR in the mid-1990s, as the college strove to draw into its fold students who demonstrated talent in domains beyond marks attained at school examinations. By 2015–16, with this process being rolled out by DU, the colleges ceded the little space for autonomy and choice they had left to centralizing tendencies within the higher education space in general.

With burgeoning numbers of admission-seekers and dizzying 'cut offs' as well as the predisposition to conflate marks at the school board examinations with 'merit', universities like DU that receive over three lakh applications a year for its undergraduate courses, perforce fall back on 'weeding out' rather than 'selecting' students. The applicant becomes an

[12]LSR was one of the few colleges that went against the tide of student protests against the Mandal Commission Report, including the self-immolation attempt by Rajeev Goswami in a strongly worded memorandum adopted by the overwhelming majority of students urging an end to violence and in support of affirmative action for socially and economically disadvantaged groups in 1990.

anonymous number, and her choice of subject and college remain as chancy as a game of roulette because of the 'one-size-fits-all' approach. The loss of voice for colleges has conspired to deprive students of avenues of considered choice.

Leveraging Space

Women's colleges have been known to deftly negotiate their 'autonomous space' while also maintaining cordial relations with the university establishment. This involves both subtle transgression and dexterous bricolage around university 'directives', and here, the equation with the vice chancellor's office and his team is crucial.

In the year 1998, when LSR conducted its own entrance examination for admission to the Commerce course, some elected representatives at DU's Academic Council raised a furore. It was later revealed that a 'favoured' candidate did not make the grade! The then vice chancellor, Prof. V.R. Mehta, having convinced himself that the college process was rigorous, fair and transparent, refused to yield to pressure or countermand the process. After he weathered the storm, his sage advice to exercise greater prudence in future was taken on board. His spirited support throughout his tenure, especially in face-offs with powerful politicians and bureaucrats over admissions, was not lost on the community, and the test was dropped the following year.

Each of the six vice chancellors with whom I had the opportunity to interact during my tenure as principal (1988–

2014) were supportive of initiatives at the women's colleges, seeing them broadly as better governed and less 'volatile' even as they brought their distinctive style and focus to administration.[13]

In terms of the percentage of women's colleges, DU, with 28.57 per cent women's colleges, compares well with the national average of approximately 10.5. Ten colleges figure in the top 40 of the National Institutional Ranking Framework (NIRF), with Miranda House and LSR making it to the top two positions in 2021, adding substantial value to DU's academic credentials. While the enrolment of women students at 42 per cent lags behind the national average of close to 49 per cent, the university has set in motion a series of initiatives to redress the skew.

The crucial interface between colleges and the university is provided by the office of the Dean of Colleges. Invariably a 'troubleshooter' for the university in its daily 'negotiations' with colleges on colliding interpretations of its 'statutes and ordinances', the dean is called upon to advise, cajole and even persuade 'recalcitrant' college administrations. The indomitable

[13]Prof. Moonis Raza (1985–90) brought a larger-than-life Nehruvian secular perspective; Upendra Baxi (1990–94) foregrounded justice, inclusion and indeed feminist perspectives; V. R. Mehta (1995–2000) fiercely protected the independence of the academy; Deepak Nayyar (2000–05) highlighted reorganization, restoration of academic reform and robust administrative practice; Deepak Pental (2005–10) emphasized promoting 'scientific temper' and propelling research; Dinesh Singh (2010–15) focussed on empowering and motivating the lesser-known colleges of the university to enhance their academic credentials.

Dr S.S. Rana, dean from 1988 to 2000, used all of these tactics, with his earthy, homespun witticisms and unmistakable warnings—depending on which college he was engaging with. He had his finger on the pulse of each constituent college and an uncanny sense of which tactics would work! His strategy with the women's colleges of DU was to nudge them along as a 'benign patriarch', familiarizing them with rules of procedure and cautioning them, often with Sanskrit parables and Vedic aphorisms, against administrative 'naivete'. This paternalistic style gave way to a more 'engendered' approach with Vice Chancellor Deepak Nayyar appointing, for the first time, two women—Kiran Datar and Hema Raghavan—as Dean of Colleges and Dean of Student Welfare, respectively, during his tenure (2000–05).

Adventure of the Quest

By its golden jubilee year in 2006, a more outward-looking LSR cast its experiential leitmotif as distinct and different. The 'magic of LSR' avowedly lay in its emphasis on:

> *Harmonizing the disciplines of structure with democratic space, the courage to take the road less travelled, redefining notions of success: creating community; resisting the monocultures of the mind, and an enlightened feminism that nurtures women confident of going beyond every glass ceiling.*[14]

[14]Report by Principal, Golden Jubilee Celebrations, 31 August 2006, Archives, Lady Shri Ram College, New Delhi.

LSR had, by now, consciously shed its 'elite' label, thanks both to national policies on reservation and affirmative action, and the focus of its own REACH programme on inclusion.[15] From 2004, the student demographic underwent a radical change. Over 65 per cent of students were non-Delhi residents, mostly from smaller towns across India—a sizeable number from economically and socially underserved backgrounds. Validating the diversity were the consistently high academic achievements. There was invariably great jubilation among students when overtaking the prestigious St. Stephen's in the *India Today* institutional rankings!

LSR's credentials as an 'engendered' space, however, had an uneven and interesting history. The question was often asked by young 'feminist' faculty and students whether the 'progressive' pronouncements of the college found adequate expression in its everyday running and experience. It appeared 'relatively easier for its Human Rights Forum to raise issues of oppression in Burma and Tibet'—it was argued—than to amend hostel rules that 'domesticate' women. How far the college 'walked its talk' was often debated.[16] Successive administrators grappled with this as they strove to balance their own responsibilities for the 'safety' of women students in

[15]The election of Lalmalswami Swamteii, an ST student from Nagaland, with an overwhelming majority in 1995 as president of the students' union reflected a significant shift in demography and student political preferences.

[16]Mohanan, Nila (ed.), Leadership with Social Responsibility: A Profile of Presidents of the Students' Union (1956-2006), Archives, Lady Shri Ram College, 2006, pp. 47–50.

the metropolis, and parental anxieties with the college's own commitment to an empowering environment. The choices were not easy, and 'caution' often proved the easier default option. Most 'progressive' HEIs confront similar dilemmas. Yet, the questioning was persistent, often irrefutable, especially when it came from young women who were accorded the right to vote at age 18 by the 61st Constitutional Amendment Act in 1989.

The college had, time and again, reiterated its mission to nurture not just 'better conformers' but women who would blaze a 'new and unusual trail', schooled in a liberating pedagogy that challenged oppressive structures of class, caste and patriarchy.[17] Navigating this terrain was an ongoing plebiscite.

Over the decades, LSR has, like most colleges, meant different things to different generations of students. Breaking free of the initial parental considerations of '*Ladki Seedhi Rahegi*' to independently 'Learn, Search and Reflect on its *Lakshya, Sadhna, Rachna*', and moving beyond the safe protection of the known and familiar in the 1980s (Let's Start a Revolution), LSR in the new millennium embraced the aphorism of 'Leadership with Social Responsibility'. It carried the audacity of hope to co-create an alternative discourse on the interconnections between a knowledge democracy and inclusive citizenship. LSR has clearly come a long way from its early moorings in 1956. How far it has crossed the rubicon

[17]Principal's Report, College Day, 1989, Archives, Lady Shri Ram College, New Delhi.

of emancipatory praxis, remains an ongoing conversation!

From the early imagination of a space that drew to its fold 'well-behaved girls' from genteel backgrounds, and shortly after, where fashionable South Delhi girls from newly rich families went, the impact of the autonomous women's movements found resonance at LSR by the late 1970s and into the 1980s, spurred by charismatic young faculty and a growing number of students eager to 'break the mould'.

By then, LSR alumnae had successfully entered the professions in large numbers—as diplomats, civil servants, lawyers, teachers and mediapersons, with many choosing careers in both corporate and voluntary sectors. From the 1990s onward, they constituted a significant number of senior scholars at universities, making an impact on quality research and the discourse on democratic inclusion. They were visible in large numbers at protests against gender-based violence.

The 'fence' between LSR and the campus became increasingly porous. Although never affiliated to the Delhi University Students Union (DUSU) and its political party loyalties, the engagement of the LSR student body with the issues at stake was informed and autonomous. LSR students held on to the view that they would not allow 'domineering stakeholders from outside' to hijack their agendas or 'wrest their voice' in the name of democracy. They had learnt to leverage their own collective weight for reform. This was in full evidence in the Think Beyond Rules (TBR) campaign in 2009, where they successfully mobilized to have a greater voice in college decision-making on student affairs. In the twenty-first century, the focus moved beyond 'glass ceilings and victimhood' to reclaiming space and voice, and assuming agentive professional leadership.

From the initial 'discovery' and discussion around Kate Millet's sexual revolution in 1971–72 to questions around a woman's identity and challenging gender stereotypes in the 1980s, issues of masculinities, marriage, family, work and constitutional rights, on to political representation, ecofeminism and violence against women in the 1990s, the palette of engagement now also includes the role of women in conflict and peace, and bodily dignity and autonomy. While the icons and templates changed over time in this fascinating trajectory, the excitement of the quest for new horizons endured!

SAKSHAM and Beyond

Faculty and students from women's colleges like LSR, among others, threw their weight behind the efforts of the intrepid Gender Study Group of DU to force the pace of 'engendering the campus' in the spirit of the Vishakha Judgment of 1997.[18] In spite of women accounting for nearly 49 per cent of total enrolment in higher education, the insouciance of HEIs in India in providing a safe and dignified work environment for women students, faculty and staff was called out in

[18]The Vishakha Judgment of the Supreme Court of India had laid down stringent guidelines for the prevention of sexual harassment at the workplace. The subsequent legislation of 2013 expanded its contours.

the ground-breaking SAKSHAM Report of the University Grants Commission in 2013.[19] It made scathing observations about the systemic violence, gendered practices, widespread misogyny and patriarchal norms prevalent within campuses. The inadequacy of basic infrastructural arrangements and civic amenities like toilets and lighting for women, sexual minorities and the differently abled, was highlighted.

The complaints about the woeful lack of amenities and facilities for women at DU were largely addressed by the restorative efforts during the tenure of Deepak Nayyar, substantially redeeming the ambience of the working environment. While concerns still remain on the 'impunity' enjoyed by some male professors, the winds of change are discernible. The culture of silence is beginning to crumble, thanks to the indefatigable women faculty who consistently hold up the mirror on the practice of invisibilizing their special needs and demands.

After Jawaharlal Nehru University (in 1999), DU was among the first to adopt a policy on sexual harassment in 2004 and formalize institutional frameworks on the structure and role

---

[19]The Report of the Gender Study Group, University of Delhi, 1996, was among the first to unambiguously highlight the necessity of regulation in the workplace to enable close to half the population of the university to work 'with dignity'. The report cited countless instances of women of campus colleges facing physical abuse and attack within the supposedly 'safe' territory of the university. See Chaudhuri, Swati, 'Three Texts, One Issue,' *Indian Journal of Gender Studies,* vol. 5, no. 1, 1998, pp. 116–21, doi: 10.1177/097152159800500108; see also SAKSHAM Report, https://bit.ly/3L9dViK. Accessed on 22 April 2022.

of complaints committees now mandated by the Act of 2013. While their efficacy is being tested every day on the ground, they did offer a useful template for implementation. DU has undoubtedly come a long way from the provocations that had spurred the iconic Vina Mazumdar of the *Towards Equality* report fame to exit the University Staff Academic Council in 1991 in protest against its inaction in a harassment case.

In India, a quiet revolution has been taking place in recent years, with unprecedented rates of growth in enrolment from social groups that even as recently as two decades ago were effectively marginalized from higher education. Women constitute a major part of this. Huge aspirations for change are being incubated in the higher education space in India. At the same time, this closing gender gap hides ongoing inequalities and disparities among women and men, which can only be gauged through an intersectional lens that combines gender with region, class, caste and religion, among others.

A Different Lens

Over 4,000 women's colleges in India—robust and thriving—have bucked the global trend of the steady decline of single-sex colleges. In the United States, their numbers have fallen from more than 300 in the first half of the twentieth century to around 35 in 2018. Here, too, several studies have shown that all-women's institutions have a vital role to play in providing a qualitatively different and more enabling environment from co-educational institutions. An increase in educational access alone does not automatically result in women's intellectual, political or social emancipation.[20] The crucial issue today is of equity.

The number of women enrolling in higher education has been rising in India by 1,350 per cent in the last seven years alone.[21] The hiring of female faculty has also substantially increased nationally from 37.85 per cent in 2010–11 to 42.5 per cent in 2019–20.[22] This is more than in any other formal sector of employment. Despite this impressive numeric increase, the absence of robust gender-just practices denies women substantive equality. Around the world, in the higher education space, the student demographic is changing in favour of women.[23] Women's institutes of higher learning

[20]See Riordan, Cornelius, 'Single- and Mixed-Gender Colleges for Women: Educational, Attitudinal, and Occupational Outcomes', *The Review of Higher Education,* vol. 15, no. 3, 1992, pp. 327–46. doi:10.1353/rhe.1992.0016; Riordan, Cornelius, 'The Value of Attending a Women's College', *The Journal of Higher Education,* vol. 65, no. 4, 1994, pp. 486–510, https://bit.ly/3xLPd3S. Accessed on 22 April 2022.

[21]Sharma, Kritika, 'Number of women enrolling in higher education rises 1,350 per cent in 7 years', *ThePrint*; 27 July 2018, https://bit.ly/3Mmwznl. Accessed on 22 April 2022.

[22]Ministry of Education, Goverment of India, *All India Survey on Higher Education 2019–20*, p. 26, https://tinyurl.com/4jmkhxzd. Accessed on 6 July 2022

[23]In the US, men are fast becoming a numerical minority on some campuses, and there is a concerted bid to boost male enrolment in colleges. See Field, Kelly, 'The Missing Men', *The Chronicle of Higher Education*, vol. 67, no. 23, 1 July 2021, https://tinyurl.com/2b4dcxfy. Accessed on 23 May 2022.

have been radically impactful in generating social capital and propelling women as change agents in the larger world that at times tends to devalue them.

A women's college is not merely an anachronistic 'room of one's own' or a 'cloistered' space that is quaintly out of date. It functions, in many ways, as an alternative civic sphere infused with powerful traditions, norms and values—sensitive to systemic exclusion and glass ceilings[24] nurturing a pedagogy that also prepares students to be worlds-ready, futures-ready and work-ready. The remarkable outreach and in-house initiatives of DU's women's colleges (Miranda House, in particular) in the face of the tectonic disruptions wrought by the pandemic foregrounded the 'ethics of care' as a much-needed paradigm for teaching–learning in an increasingly uncertain world. They signalled that 'engendering' the academy requires expanding 'empathetic' and 'healing' spaces.

Several women's colleges at DU, especially over the last decade, have moved beyond their (self) perception as 'safe spaces' to 'brave spaces'. Some of them consciously deploy feminist pedagogy to do several things differently. Teaching strategies facilitate a more 'constructivist' classroom, recognize that learning is cognitive, dialogic and experiential, and connect with the lived realities of the learner. They acknowledge the fluidity and multiplicity of identities, and employ collaborative

---

[24]Speech by Joanne V. Creighton, President, Mount Holyoke College, 'Public Advocacy and Women's Education', Bellagio Conference on Women's Education World Wide, 22–24 August, 2007.

teaching–learning strategies that contextualize course material.[25] Women's colleges have displayed an impressive track record in campus diversity initiatives strong in 'social activism' and (altruistic) community orientation[26], significantly altering the grammar of success. Scholar bell hooks's ideas about 'teaching to transgress'[27] and education as the practice of freedom, with the classroom as a space to fundamentally rethink democratic participation, find resonance here.

Such pedagogies challenge ethnocentric, anthropocentric and androcentric constructions of knowledge, muscular power hierarchies and exclusionary notions of merit. They seek international linkages as a context to transcend cartographic anxieties, to receive from and contribute to the intellectually diverse Learning Commons. They strive to nurture global citizens, cultures of peace and the canvas of coexistence. They connect with people's movements that seek to expand the contours of informed citizenship.

The academy, today, is a fluid daily plebiscite contingent on how it navigates an array of choices, such as between academic freedom and organizational accountability; between

---

[25]Langdon, Emily A., 'Women's Colleges Then and Now, Access Then, Equity Now', *Peabody Journal of Education,* vol. 76, no. 1, 2001, pp. 5–30, https://bit.ly/3vAY6uH. Accessed on 22 April 2022.

[26]Kim, Mikyong Minsun, 'Institutional Effectiveness of Women-only Colleges: Cultivating Students' Desire to Influence Social Conditions', *The Journal of Higher Education,* vol. 72, no. 3, 2001, pp. 310–11, https://bit.ly/3Mrt1QX. Accessed on 22 April 2022.

[27]hooks, bell, *Teaching to Transgress: Education as the Practice of Freedom,* Routledge, New York, 1994.

its connection with the State and centres of power and the need to maintain strategic distance; between equality, inclusion and international benchmarks of performance; between teaching as the transmission of critical attitudes and society's expectations on qualifications for employability; between contributing to the economy and 'providing a space free from utilitarian pressures'[28]; between the proximate classroom and the digital universe; between the transmission of established knowledge and opening new horizons of thought; and between connecting beyond borders and preserving 'national culture' and identity.

It is within this mosaic that DU must calibrate its autonomy, recast its priorities and celebrate its distinctive identity.

The current engagement and evolving aspirations of DU's women's colleges invoke the Proustian wisdom that the 'real voyage of discovery consists not in seeking new landscapes but in having new eyes.' By speaking in a different voice, do they also provide us with the conceptual alphabets for a new vocabulary of learning, knowing and being that will propel DU in its hundredth year?

The tide…it is a-turning…as the river renews itself.

---

[28]See Anderson, Robert, 'The "Idea of a University" Today', History and Policy (H&P), online papers, 1 March 2010, https://bit.ly/3EDjJ1h. Accessed on 22 April 2022.

INTEGRATION AND ASPIRATION

Kiren Rijiju

University is where you become your own person, get defined as an individual and develop beliefs that you carry forward for the rest of your life. And Delhi University did exactly that for me and thousands of other students, generation after generation.

As this glorious institution celebrates 100 years today, I pondered over the three years I spent at Hansraj College first and then the years spent earning my law degree at the Faculty of Law.

So, how did my years in DU define me apart from providing world-class education? The answer to this question may not be easy.

Today's youth may not get what I am saying, so allow me to paint a rather nostalgic picture for you. Imagine a time when telephones were a luxury, a printed photograph often captured a lifetime's memory and 'technology' meant newspapers, radio and State television. Now, picture a youth who had come from a tribal family living in the small village of Nafra in the northeastern-most state of Arunachal Pradesh to India's bustling capital city—a youth with many dreams, but all unwoven and unplanned, and yet, underpinned by a motivation of wanting to be of service to our great country.

India's best campuses have always been a melting pot, and it was no different when I arrived in college. At a time when mainland India was still learning new facts and ideas about the Northeast and shedding prejudices, the DU campus was years ahead. I never felt like an 'outsider' in the university, and truth be told, I never allowed anyone to treat me like that too. From teachers and librarians to canteen staff and janitors, no one saw me as different from any other.

At that moment in life, I realized that India as a nation does not have to be 'different' for each of us; it just has to be for all of us. I would go on record to say that DU's contribution in including Northeast students to the mainland conversation and ideas is second to none. Every Northeast student who studies at DU, I believe, becomes richer in thought, ideas and humanity.

Undoubtedly, DU campuses often bring the best out of India's mind-boggling diversity: a Malayali could have a Naga roommate, attend a Kashmiri teacher's class and then accompany his friends to eat Punjabi food. Every day, you learn, unlearn and relearn something new about the world, and even yourself. Notwithstanding this diversity, in DU, we were all equal, just as in India, we are all equal. Many years later, this same feeling was encapsulated by our Hon'ble Prime Minister Narendra Modi when he coined the phrase '*Sabka Saath, Sabka Vikas*'.

All the World's a Stage

As a student, I was taught the value of cultural activities, and at the cost of self-promotion, allow me to say that I was a good athlete too. And you do not need me to tell you that sport has no language, thereby ensuring that no matter where we came from, if we knew a sport, we knew how and what to talk about. All this helped me find common causes and shared bonds with those in my college.

It was, therefore, not surprising that barely a year into college came the defining moment of my university life—representing India as a member of the youth and cultural team that participated in the Festival of India in USSR in 1987. This was a singular honour in recognition of my efforts in my student days. It also gave me self-confidence and belief in my own enterprise as well as the realization that Indians were not effectively showcasing their cultural quotient at a global level. I ensured that India and its youth stood tall at a big, international stage.

Back home, I excelled on yet another stage—the political one. After all, let us not forget that politics was second nature to DU—a university that has always remained politically vibrant and energized right from the post-Independence days and especially through the dark days of the Emergency. DU allowed new entrants like me—who do not belong to rich and powerful families such as the one running the country at the time—the space to make our voices heard.

I was an active member of the Akhil Bharatiya Vidyarthi

Parishad (ABVP) in my college days and campaigned aggressively. The lessons I learnt on party mobilization, unity and political organizations were better than any book that I could have picked up on the subject. Politics, I learnt, would only be successful if it is truly in service of people and society.

I might sound old here, but I do believe that in those days, there was a lot of attention paid to conversations. The debates, often fiery, shaped me as a person and also as a politician. DU taught me that political adversaries could sit and debate for hours yet care deeply for each other. In Parliament, it is common for political rivals to share a laugh, a hug or talk to each other as equals. I am sure I will not be alone when I say this: the role of DU in shaping the political affairs that have, in turn, shaped India, is both exemplary and undeniable.

As DU marks 100 glorious years, we are at an extremely crucial juncture in India's history. Under the visionary leadership of Shri Narendra Modiji, India's stature on the world stage, especially in a post-pandemic world, has never been higher. It is our responsibility to continue to strive together. I once again remind myself of the lessons I learnt during my days at DU. Every day we learn, and every day we grow.

TRIALS, TRAVAILS AND TRIUMPHS AT JMC

Namita Gokhale

This is the tale of a troubled but rewarding chapter of my life. The year was 1972. I was 16, and among the youngest in my class when I passed of out of Mater Dei Convent in December 1971. Our school was often referred to as 'Matar Dahi Convent'; it was conventional and strict, but I have happy memories of it. I had received admission to Miranda House, Lady Shri Ram College (LSR) as well as the recently established Jesus and Mary College (JMC) in Chanakyapuri (St. Stephen's College only opened its doors to women students in 1975).

I was strangely drawn to the peace and quiet of JMC, to the birdsong and the banks of bougainvillea, and the large, well-lit library. The college was affiliated to the South Campus. Several of my school friends enrolled there, as did I. Little did I know or imagine the deep impact this decision would leave on the rest of my life.

It was exhilarating to be young and full of hope. So many adventures awaited all of us. We were not so world-weary as today's generation. Books. Films. Travel. Boys. There was so much to learn, so much to look forward to. Some snapshots from memory: sashaying down a makeshift ramp and tripping over my cotton sari as I was crowned first runner-up in the Miss JMC Contest. Catching the Ladies Special to the college, with a busload of happy, giggling, carefree girls. The library, where I was always the first to find my perch. The teachers—a brilliant and committed lot. Muriel Wasi, Shobhana Bhattacharjee, Malashri Lal and so many others—opening our eyes to the wonders of focused literary appreciation.

Looking back so many years later, I recall the sense of calm, of expectancy, of vast expanse. Brisk mornings, golden afternoons. I wanted to study philology and become an academic. It was all planned out, meant to unroll as smoothly as a red carpet. If I didn't meet the man of my dreams by the time I was 27, I would have an arranged marriage. Twenty-seven felt impossibly old, over the hill—I was still just 16.

We often wore saris, me and my friends, not because we had to but because we loved the texture and drape of the cotton. It was the *Guddi* look, inspired by the young Jaya Bhaduri. The default mode was bell bottoms, favoured by both boys and girls. The boys usually sported sideburns and lived in a haze of idealism. They smoked and smoked up a lot, and talked of Keynesian economics and strummed at guitars.

Delhi University seemed a different universe, with a different pace, a different vocabulary. I had a group of friends who were boys—not quite boyfriends—in St. Stephen's College. There was the iconic *Kooler Talk*, with its sometimes indecipherable jokes. The boys from Hindu College and Shri Ram College of Commerce (SRCC) were distinct in their vocabulary, their attitudes, and through so many other intangible markers. The Miranda House girls were different too, more 'cool', more radical and more independent than us JMC-types. As for the girls from the LSR, they were on another level altogether in their determination and focus. Looking back, I reflect on how each college had such a distinctive identity, each reflecting the personalities and dedication of their distinct and distinguished faculty who invested so much of themselves in the teaching profession.

The year is now 1973. I was older but not really much wiser. I was 17 and wading my way through exciting discoveries and hurtful betrayals. I came second in the university in English literature that year, and it felt good. I was in awe of Shakespeare and enchanted by Dickens, but the sheen of English literature was wearing off. It seemed distanced in its vocabulary and subtext from the life around me. I had encountered the plays of Mohan Rakesh, seen them enacted at the All India Fine Arts and Crafts Society theatre, which was not far from where I lived. I was deeply impacted by *Ghashiram Kotwal*, by Vijay Tendulkar, performed in Hindi. I had seen *Tughlaq* by Girish Karnad being staged against the magnificent ramparts of Purana Qila, with the legendary actor Manohar Singh playing the lead. I had discovered the literary power of my mother tongue, sensed the creative excitement as contemporary writers, playwrights and actors reinterpreted their times.

The college elections were to be held. The vice president was elected from amongst the second-year students, while the president was from the third year. I decided to stand for vice president, and to my surprise, was elected unopposed. My dear friend Louise Fernandes, a year senior to me and who was also studying English literature, was elected as president. Later, Louise starred in a college production of George Bernard Shaw's *Pygmalion*, with Salman Khurshid from St. Stephen's in the male lead as Professor Henry Higgins. It was a delightfully staged play with an even more delightful aftermath. Louise and Salman fell in love and were married some years later.

That was also the year I met Rajiv Gokhale, the person I was to marry when I turned 18. He had successfully evaded classes at SRCC and was due to graduate soon. He would pick me up after college, and I would spend time with him learning about photography and films. We would argue about UFOs and aliens. He was a believer; I was not. We planned to set up a magazine together, and I had my first introduction to publishing by simply jumping into the deep end.

We got married in the summer of 1974. I was 18, he was 20. My father-in-law, H.R. Gokhale, was the minister of law and justice in Indira Gandhi's Cabinet. Mother Aquinas Vegas, the stern Kerala nun who was the then principal of JMC, did not approve of my decision. She had asked to be introduced to Rajiv. When they met, the chemistry was not good. They had gotten into an argument about Class IV employees who were on strike and picketing outside the college at the time.

A Crisis and a Change of Direction

I still dreamt of studying comparative philology, of learning Sanskrit and Latin, and excavating the roots and words and the sources from where they derived their meanings. But life had other plans, as did a strangely disposed nun in JMC. In my third year of college, disillusioned by the Anglo-centric 'Eng. Lit.' curriculum, I decided to opt for a new option that DU was offering, in Modern Indian Literature (MIL), where I could study selected contemporary Hindi writers. The course was offered as an alternative to the paper on Chaucer and Old English, and sounded infinitely more alluring. Nobody I knew had actually taken the option, but it all seemed straightforward enough. I would prepare for paper 8B on my own, and informed Dr Malashri Lal—the teacher who taught us Chaucer—of my decision.

I had to study the course myself and could not mark myself present or get attendance for the hours spent in the library. Mother Aquinas must have been aware of my decision but did not comment on it at that time. However, while filling in the examination form, I was summoned to her office to be told that I could not sit for the examination for paper 8B, as I had not been taught it. The days that followed were full of further shocks. The principal held back over a hundred students, refusing to accept their medical certificates or their reasons for absence. I, too, fell into this category because of my having opted for the alternative paper.

Chaos and crisis have followed me through my life, often leading to unexpected and even positive outcomes. Looking back today, almost 50 years later, I realize that the principal's decision was possibly the most pivotal challenge I ever faced. In the months that followed, my dreams of academia, of becoming Dr Namita Gokhale, were shattered forever. I was led instead on another path altogether. The students who had been held back met up with my sister-in-law Sunanda Bhandare, a popular and distinguished lawyer who was later to become a judge of the Delhi High Court. It was clear that Mother Aquinas was not going to relent from her stand, and Sunanda advised that they should seek relief from the courts. She would represent them pro bono.

Arun Jaitley, the president of the students' union of DU, argued on our behalf. Kumkum Khanna And Ors. vs The Mother Acquinas And Anr. was to become a much-cited case on the issue of academic freedom and discipline. The Delhi High Court was still situated in Patiala House in those days. I remember the palpable excitement that rippled through the courtroom as it filled up with a bevy of chattering girls. Justices V.S. Deshpande and Yogeshwar Dayal gave a patient and sympathetic hearing to our case as they pondered whether the principal of a private college recognized by the university was justified in being bound by her own administrative policy.

The court directed the principal to give a special hearing to several of the petitioners. In my case, they ruled 'We, therefore, set aside the order of detention against the petitioner and direct the Principal to give her a hearing.' I had also made a representation to the vice chancellor and the Academic Council to consider my situation, as the matter of paper 8B was outside the jurisdiction of the principal.

We were given permission to appear in the examination. I enjoyed answering the question paper, which I remember had some incisive questions on *Vaishali Ki Nagarvadhu* by Acharya Chatursen Shastri as well as the plays of Mohan Rakesh. But, despite taking the examination, the results were never declared. As a minority institution, JMC could be advised by the Delhi High Court but was not bound to follow the advice. Mother Aquinas failed to follow up the nudge from the courts and refused to exercise the discretion vested with her to officially clear us, even though the court had allowed us to sit for the examination.

In the meanwhile, the Emergency had been declared. Arun Jaitley, who had advised me to appeal to the vice chancellor and the Academic Council, had gone underground. I decided then to forget about formal education and live and learn on my own terms in the real world. I didn't return to JMC to repeat the year, as many of my friends and classmates did. I was to remain a student all my life, learning where and what I could, but my days at DU were over.

So much for comparative philology and my dreams of academia! I realize now that the most important lessons are learnt outside the classroom. Instead of returning to college, I set up a film magazine called *Super*, where I learnt the fundamentals of publishing on the job. If I had graduated, as I so desperately wanted to, I may never have begun my writing career in 1984 with *Paro: Dreams of Passion*, my debut novel, which broke all the rules, adopting a rebellious streak that I perhaps picked up at the university. Another of my novels, *The Book of Shadows*, has a dramatic and tragic opening interlude set in JMC, the same college that rejected me.

Life is full of ironies. Mother Aquinas was called to Rome but decided to leave the Church some years later. I wonder if she ever realized what an impact she had had on the course my life was to take, before she renounced her vocation. Life is also cyclical. I have co-edited two books with Dr Malashri Lal, and co-authored a play with her. Of all my teachers in JMC, I had been closest to her. Our lives followed very different trajectories; hers, a distinguished academic career; mine, an up-and-down life of trials and travails, challenges and triumphs. Our love of literature held us together, and the journey we began in a bougainvillea-covered campus has continued, in unexpected directions, as often happens in the journey of life.

I have had the privilege of continuing my passion for the Indian languages and their literatures by showcasing them at the Jaipur Literature Festival (JLF), of which I am the co-founder and co-director. Life has come full circle.

I am not a graduate and I am proud of it. I studied in DU and I am proud of that too. My two daughters are also alumni of the same university, and I am proud of that too. I consider it one of the most grounded, generous and liberal institutions anywhere.

THE START OF STARTING UP

Vijay Shekhar Sharma

The year 1994 was when I got into the Delhi College of Engineering (DCE; Delhi Technological University or DTU now) for a BTech degree in electronics and communications—feels like a lifetime ago. Yet, the learnings, memories and friendships I formed in those four years continue to stay close to my heart even today. I arrived from Harduaganj, near Aligarh, and was ready to start a journey in the big, affluent city of Delhi, carrying not just my own dreams but also that of my entire family (if not also my school and town).

It was overwhelming to be the first student from my school to have made it to DCE, let alone being the youngest in my batch at 15 years. All these achievements were enough for me to set foot inside the arched gates of DCE with the confidence of Super Mario. And to the extent that it could embrace a dreamy-eyed townie like me, DCE embraced me with open arms. There was a sense of freedom in being so far away from home, of being able to explore a city I had heard and read so much about. Even the constant blowing of horns was music to my ears, crossing busy roads, a new-found challenge, and everything in between, a new experience.

At the same time, I missed the sleepiness of my town's evenings as well as my mother's guiding voice. On a more fundamental level, the difference between the staidness of my town and the ferocious pace of Delhi came to symbolize a deep divide—one in which I was now ensnared as much as by my own expectation as by the realization that I was 'different' from my peers. The manicured lawns of the university represented this divergence between me and those around me. I looked around, almost hopelessly, as young boys in 'cooler' clothing debated and joked around with each other in English as they lounged on the grass. Their body language, gestures and words were all so unfamiliar. And here I was, from a Hindi-medium school, struggling to grasp the fast-racing words of English. The subjects were taught in English, the textbooks, too, were in English, but it might as well have been in Greek and Latin. Every letter that the teacher spoke or wrote on the blackboard flew off the board, over my head and out of the door.

When I was preparing for the engineering entrance examination, I used to sit down with two language versions of the same book at the same time, but conversing and understanding sentences, that too when spoken so fast, was a different ballgame altogether. So, with every passing week, I descended to the back of the classroom and finally out of it. But not far, though. I found my solace in DCE's well-equipped Computer Centre that became my new classroom. I would spend hours familiarizing myself with computers and all that they had to offer, and discovering new things every day. An electronics engineering student addicted to the computer!

That is when I realized that DCE didn't just push me towards the dreams that I had arrived with, instead, it gave me new wings to fly, it gave me access to a whole new world—one where I found my footing. There was space for every interest to grow and flourish at DU, even of a 15-year-old boy who struggled to grasp the language and the culture of the place. Even as I was catching up with my course subjects, I would use the facilities available to nourish my interest in computers and carve a parallel path.

What helped in my assimilation into the university was the fact that I was exposed to a gamut of students from diverse backgrounds. Nowhere else in India does one get to see such diversity. Their diverse experiences and ideas helped me broaden my understanding of people. My worldview underwent a complete transformation. Instead of withdrawing myself as a result of the exclusion I had felt early on in campus, I realized that there was much to be learned from everyone in my college and the university. This, of course, happened most acutely in my hostel, where I had more time to converse and socialize with my batchmates and seniors alike. I found a place for myself in those interactions and experiences, and before I had even begun to understand it, I had inserted myself into the cultural spaces of the college.

37, Kash Gate and Beyond

Initially, East Hostel and its residents were again an alien world for me. The boys were freewheeling, so confident, so bindaas. They exuded freedom in the way I had never felt or seen before. But in Room No. 37, East Hotel, DCE, Kashmere Gate (my room), I was introduced to my first love—music! My hostel-mates would play music from different parts of the world, and soon it became our favourite pastime. It was in East Hostel that I first heard my favourite bands—U2 and Coldplay. Inspiration comes from the strangest places—in Bono, I found my English teacher, and there were many such rock-band frontmen whose words became my Wren and Martin. I would learn the lyrics and play them back in my head in a loop. If books and computers sucked me in, music pulled my heart's strings.

And in those corridors of the hostel, I formed some of my strongest friendships—born out of pure innocence. They were unhindered and non-judgemental (and remain so even today), so much so that once when browsing through a magazine with my friend Harinder Thakar in computer class I came across the word 'notebook' used for a certain type of laptop, I let a silly question escape my mouth. '*Notebook to wo hota hai na jispe hum pen se likh sakte hain* (Isn't notebook one in which we write with a pen)?' I had asked. He had a hearty laugh but was kind enough to explain the difference.

Another friend told me about the goldmine that was the Daryaganj book market, where one could buy tattered second-hand books for a pittance. For me, I had hit a bigger jackpot! In one of those quests to find second-hand English magazines, I stumbled upon some issues of *Fortune*, *Forbes* and *NetGuide*. In those issues, I discovered Silicon Valley in the midst of the roaring 1990s and the boom of this glorious new thing called the internet. There, in the pages of a hand-me-down magazine, I came across Jerry Yang's Yahoo, and Marc Andreessen's Netscape, even as I devoured the many other inspiring stories of tech entrepreneurship.

These stories sowed the seeds of entrepreneurship in me. So, with Harinder and two other friends and 'Red Hill Mining Town' by U2 blasting in the background—the tech company 'XS Corps—The Internet Giant' was founded. The lyrics of the song went 'You're all that's left to hold on to… I'm still waiting… I'm hanging on… You're all that's left to hold on to', and we felt that it was speaking to us because the survival of XS Corps meant our survival. XS Corps was born in our hostel room, or as we called it in youthful abandon, '37, Kash Gate'. The rooms and corridors of the hostel became our Silicon Valley. It is where I discovered myself and what I wanted to do with my life.

What also helped me were the various cultural and technical clubs and societies in the university. These societies were a place and platform for demonstrating one's passion and interest through practical experience. It was an opportunity for juniors to learn from the expertise of their seniors on various subjects. It also polished our organizational and negotiating skills. The college authorities were also generous enough to let us use the computers without restrictions on time or usage. I was hooked on to programming and building XS Corps to live up to its tagline.

We sold XS Corps to Living Media soon after we got out of college in 1998, by when we had managed to clock ₹50 lakh in revenue. Here, in the campus of DCE, I had my first brush with entrepreneurship, one that taught me that success will come to you, but not without a long road of hardships.

Rewriting the India Story

Today, when I look back, I realize how all these experiences culminated into making me the person that I am. When faced with tough situations, we often tend to dwell upon the problem instead of finding a solution. However, I was able to stop focusing on my weaknesses and channel my energies into something more positive and productive. I did not want to be defined by the fact that I didn't know a language. And the atmosphere at DCE afforded me the zeal to go beyond my limitations. I sometimes think to myself how my life would have turned out had I not stumbled into the Computer Centre. I have carried with me the principles of the DU motto—*Nishtha, Dhriti, Satyam* (dedication, steadfastness and truth)—all through these years, and have always been rewarded for abiding by them.

In DU, I had seen people from all walks of life around me. I was myself from a lower-middle-class family in a small town.

That is the beauty of India. In its diversity and equitable roots, Indian education has laid the path of dignity and prosperity for every Indian. I hope that readers who find resonance with my humble beginnings might take some solace and a much bigger dollop of inspiration from my story.

There is a very short poem I had written when I was 12:

Main garibi hoon;
main tumse pyaar karti hoon;
main tumhe chhod nahin sakti,
kyunki tum mujhse jyada pyar karte ho!

I had wanted to convey the importance of self-as-enterprise. There is no situation that we cannot get ourselves out of—even poverty—if we grab the opportunities that we make for ourselves or are available to us.

The infrastructure of DCE enabled students to flourish. We were allowed to be our own person, pursue our interests without hindrance and carve our own paths. Dreaming big was nobody's fiefdom nor was support scarce for the ones who asked. To all the youngsters who are at DCE today, you should know that you are in a space that allows you to harbour your dreams. While you are at it, dream and dream big.

My time at DCE also taught me the importance of working as a team. Of course, back then, the team meant your 'gang', i.e. your circle of friends. I suspect it is much the same even today. Having each other's back, helping each other grow and standing by each other through all odds are life lessons that I have learnt from my time at DCE.

Though the entrepreneurship journey can be very lonely and extremely daunting, if one has managed to create a team—like a gang in college—much of their burden is reduced. Today, I am fortunate enough to get to work with some of my college-mates. The relationships forged in college have stayed with me, and DU's education has ensured all of us emerged as fine professionals equipped to produce world-class companies, products and services.

My own wave of entrepreneurship with Paytm has come with its own highs and lows. DCE taught me that when faced with even the largest wave, it is your choice whether you will run from it or ride it. Failures are a part of life, there is no escaping them. It is the fear of failure, though, that needs to be overcome first. It is something I have learnt from my passion for adventure sports, especially rafting. The first rapids are the scariest, but once you tide over it, the subsequent ones don't terrify anymore. It becomes fun instead. Have faith and believe in your dreams. Believe that no matter where you come from, there are multitudes of places that you can go. But as you walk, leave an indelible mark of making a difference in the lives of the underserved. With Paytm, this is what we are attempting to do—take digital payments and financial services to every corner of India and be a part of the Indian's growth story.

When I was in college, a handful of us dreamt of becoming entrepreneurs, but now the start-up culture has become part of everyday discourse. Universities, too, have become huge enablers of the entrepreneurial mindset and ecosystem. Seize that opportunity! Listen to diverse voices. The quietest student in your class might have a brilliant idea or input to offer. My story, like the story of hundreds of others from DU, is evidence of the fact.

What you learn as students in DU today will lay the foundation of the role you play as leaders and creators tomorrow. And together, we can rewrite the India story and etch our country's name in the history books of tomorrow as a nation that taught the world what the finest experience of technology looks like.

THE THREE DEFINING CONFLICTS THAT SHAPED MY LIFE

Hardeep S. Puri

It was a hot summer forenoon in 1968. I stood on Delhi University's Imperial Avenue (now Sudhir Bose Marg), on either side of which are situated two of its premier institutions: Hindu College, where I spent five years—three years as an undergraduate student and two years as a postgraduate student, though classes were not held in the college but in the university itself—and St. Stephen's College, where I spent a year as a member of the teaching faculty. On that summer day, it was not the sultry heat that was affecting me but a sense of anxiety—unease bordering on nervousness. I stood there, all of 16 years of age, with a school-leaving certificate and some other documentation attesting to my proficiency in sports and other extracurricular activities. I had applied for admission to the undergraduate course in History Honours in several DU colleges. The first two interview calls came from these institutions and, coincidentally, were slotted one after the other.

My first interview was in St. Stephen's College. Most of

the talking was done by Professor Mohammad Amin, widely respected as an excellent teacher with phenomenal memory, who also happened to be a raconteur of a very high order. He had settled into a relatively relaxed life of academics, sports and administration, without undertaking the rigour of further research and a PhD.

My interview that morning did not go well. He quizzed me on my so-called 'achievements'. I was left with the distinct impression that my academic credentials and whatever I had to show by way of extracurricular activities did not impress him particularly. Anything I said in response to a question resulted in the bar being raised. Invariably, the questions appeared to be designed to suggest that I had either not fully exploited my potential or that I did not have the credentials to qualify for admission to St. Stephen's. I am mentioning this in some detail only because there was a delicious irony in another interaction five years later that had starkly different results.

Immediately after this somewhat unnerving experience, I walked across the road to Hindu College where I was interviewed by the head of the History Department, Professor Bipan Chandra. The author of *The Rise and Growth of Economic Nationalism in India*, Chandra was a teacher who became a legend in his own lifetime. His stints at Stanford and Delhi were followed by an equally illustrious tenure at JNU where he was also appointed Professor Emeritus. The tone, tenor and content of the interview was entirely different, and from my point of view, a fascinating eye-opener.

He did not appear fixated on academic 'achievements' or

the mark sheet as well as the testimonials on extracurricular activities and sports that my application folder contained. He, instead, wished to have a short chat on any topic of my interest or related to any activity other than academic that I had participated in recently. He even suggested that we could discuss that morning's newspaper headlines and said I should feel free to make any suggestion in terms of the subject that I would like to discuss.

I ventured to suggest that I had enjoyed debating and dramatics whilst in school. He asked me what plays, if any, I had acted in. On hearing that I had played Mark Antony in *Julius Caesar*, he wanted me to recite something from the play. I decided to shun the oft-quoted 'Friends, Romans, countrymen…' monologue. Instead, I delivered, verbatim, the concluding part of the funeral oration, reciting the following from memory:

> **Antony**: Moreover, he hath left you all his walks,
> His private arbours and new-planted orchards,
> On this side Tiber; he hath left them you,
> And to your heirs for ever; common pleasures,
> To walk abroad, and recreate yourselves.
> Here was a Caesar: When comes such another?
>
> **First Citizen**: Never, never! Come, away, away!
> We'll burn his body in the holy place,
> And with the brands fire the traitors' houses.
> Take up the body.
>
> **Second Citizen**: Go, fetch fire.

Third Citizen: Pluck down benches.

Fourth Citizen: Pluck down forms, windows, any thing.

Antony: Now let it work. Mischief, thou art afoot,
Take thou what course thou wilt!

The rest of the interview lasted less than three minutes. He asked me whether I wished to seriously pursue academics, or also participate in debating, dramatics and sports. I replied, 'Academics and debating.' When I topped DU in history in 1971, he recalled our conversation. After I got a first in MA, he called me to say he was confident I would do well in academics, if I chose to make that a profession.

A World outside of Textbooks

What makes a university? Clearly, the quality of the teaching faculty and the administration make a significant contribution. Equally, students should possess and demonstrate thirst for knowledge and dedication to the art of learning itself—all anchored within an overall intellect to be able to both absorb and contribute. In the ultimate analysis, this becomes a little like the 'chicken and egg story'. One of DU's premier colleges has a tradition where old students who have done well and made a mark for themselves are invited to address an after-dinner gathering. In a desire to be gracious and express gratitude to the institution that had shaped this gentleman's life, one alumnus inscribed, 'I am what I am because of the college.' Another alumnus, perhaps only to have a little fun, inscribed, 'Why blame the college?'

In the late 1960s, when my generation entered university, entry requirements were not particularly stringent. It is entirely possible that the approach to education was different. Hindu College was clearly willing to admit students who did not have the highest of scores in 1968, when I received my admission. By contrast, the undergraduate classes in Hindu College in the academic year 2021–22 witnessed students in the general category requiring to obtain 99.5 per cent marks or higher in their school-leaving certificates to secure admission in the first list of BA (Hons.) History and 100 per cent marks for BA (Hons.) Political Science at the college![1] A feat impossible even to imagine back in 1968.

The high calibre of the teaching faculty and the conducive environment for learning were instrumental in my doing well academically. Life outside academics was equally enjoyable. I was among the leading debaters in DU, having led Hindu College to victory in the prestigious Mukarji Memorial debate competition three years in a row. I was also heavily involved in student politics and was elected the prime minister of the college parliament in 1970–71. I proudly remember that Professor Premchand, a legendary teacher and stalwart educationalist who was the speaker of the Hindu College Parliament, had predicted that I'd get 'more votes than the other candidates combined' after listening to my election speech, which I did.

I believe these non-academic endeavours were catalytic

[1]Hindu College, 'First Cut-Off List (04.10.2021–07.10.2021)', https://tinyurl.com/mr7tkzxc. Accessed on 7 July 2022.

factors in my development. The myriad opportunities the university provided me to push myself enabled me to become a better articulator and an empathetic decision-maker. Various encounters and experiences helped develop strong analytical skills and a penchant for persuasion that paid rich dividends in later life. Hindu College in the late 1960s and early 1970s had a distinctive vibe. The college, which always set itself apart from others in DU, reflected the determination and the anger of the youth. The tradition of the college, steeped in its nationalistic roots, combined with the explosion of anti-establishment feeling in the early 1970s to alchemize a unique experience that was entirely outside of textbooks. It was a happening time, especially for the idealistic generation of students that I belonged to.

When I completed my master's, fate once again brought me to an interview at St. Stephen's with the chair of the governing body, the principal and Prof. Amin. This time, I was invited by the college to apply for a teaching position for the academic year 1973–74. I am glad to say that this second interview had a far more pleasant outcome. If memory serves me correctly, I replaced Robi Chatterjee (who had gone on a sabbatical to Cambridge) as the lecturer, a job that paid ₹400 a month. The arc of my life at DU makes me laugh even today. It began with an interview at St. Stephen's and ended with one at St. Stephen's. Irony works in strange ways.

This is an appropriate juncture to consider the core of my rumination—the three major conflicts that I experienced at DU:

1. academia versus livelihood;
2. the 'real' India: truths versus dominant narratives; and
3. a personal intellectual framework versus continuing with a colonial mindset.

These three conflicts, I believe, have directed the course of my life ever since. Originating in my experiences at the university, these three conflicts have stayed with me in my ongoing study of continuity and change of sociopolitical affairs that I have encountered in various personas—as a student of history, and in my career as a diplomat, bureaucrat, politician and minister. It is no exaggeration to say that these interwoven conflicts have been essential in moulding my worldview. Many readers will relate, to varying degree, with my experiences.

Academia versus Livelihood

It was fortuitous that I had the opportunity to teach at St. Stephen's. At the time, I might well have settled into a comfortable but perhaps less exciting life in academia. Life might have taken a different route had I been offered a permanent vacancy on the teaching staff, but that was not to be. William Shaw Rajpal, who was the then principal of St. Stephen's, wanted me to continue teaching at the college but declined to give me a permanent position at the time. He feared that I would write the UPSC examination as I continued to teach—a common strategy adopted by young lecturers in DU at the time. Faced with the prospect of being unemployed a year later encouraged me to take the plunge.

I did well in the UPSC examination and was selected to the Indian Foreign Service (IFS) in 1974 in the first attempt itself. I was among the youngest in my batch and went on to serve the government for a record 39 years.

Back then, those who had the choice went to work at a few select positions that brought with them security and respectability. India was stuck in a low-growth equilibrium in the early 1970s. There were limited opportunities in the closed, socialist Indian economy, which depended almost entirely on the State and its institutions. Graduates from DU who did well academically and otherwise would either opt for the Tata Administrative Services (TAS), the State Bank of India (SBI), Hindustan Unilever (HUL), or would write a government examination. Those were the only realistic choices. There was a traditional DU refrain: if you passed in the First Division, you either went into research or became an IAS officer; if you passed in the Second Division, you went into business; and if you passed in the Third Division, you became a lawyer. Of course, there were many notable exceptions.

Jocularity aside, the refrain should impress upon the reader the sparseness of options young students had in the 1970s. This coincided with the lower-middle-class backgrounds of most students, which forced them to prioritize 'dependable' jobs in government or highly established industry/PSU positions. In a nutshell, this was my first conflict. What were the choices I had when confronted with the very real conundrum of earning a livelihood?

I came from a lower-middle-class family whose upward

mobility was founded on education. My great-grandfather held the prestigious post of 'Civil Surgeon' in British India. My grandfathers, both paternal and maternal, were educationists. My father and his brother became civil servants. With the benefit of hindsight, this was more due to the unsettling of their lives on account of Partition rather than the exercise of a choice or preference. Nevertheless, their success laid the foundation for me to reap the full benefits of opportunity. Education enabled my family to journey from travelling by cycle to travelling in a car in my lifetime alone. It helped avoid the devastating effects of Partition. I was born only a few years after Partition, but the respectable standing of my family helped me excel as well.

And yet, research and academia, despite my ardent interest, seemed options of luxury. Studying further—just for the sake of it—was viewed as a frivolous indulgence. I was a good student who had done very well in college. I narrowly missed out on the Rhodes Scholarship. Had I received the scholarship, things might have been different. Even after I joined the IFS, my desire to take up something in academia persisted. I took up evening classes to study law after my stint in Tokyo but could not continue to devote time to it because of existing work and familial commitments. Again, had I been able to pursue studies beyond my master's degree, things might have turned out differently.

This dilemma was the crux of my first conflict. I had to forsake desire for pragmatism. How many others felt like me? I believe I speak for an entire generation that was lost to the finiteness of opportunity in the post-Independence era. Ours was not the 'lost generation' that Gertrude Stein referred to when she spoke of the post-World War I generation, but it was definitely an 'inhibited generation' that was not allowed to realize much of its creativity and potential. Today's youth has it different: they have a plethora of options to choose from—just as it should be. Young Indians, especially Indian women, are breaking down barriers and charting new avenues in today's promising environment to explore options not just in academia but also in entrepreneurship and various social disciplines.

The 'Real' India: Truths versus Dominant Narratives

The second conflict that I experienced at DU arose when I tried to reconcile my upbringing in an Anglo-Indian denominational school with the Indian multitude that I experienced at Hindu College. The former was representative of an orthodox Christian environment: by and large, muted, elite and 'proper' when it was not catering to its programmes for inclusion of the relatively marginalized members of the Anglo-Indian community. The latter was brimming with cultural and ethnic diversity that spanned the spectrum of class, religion and caste. Had I gone to St. Stephen's instead of 'the college across the road', perhaps the conflict may not have been as pronounced. I would have remained ignorant, for a while longer, of the chasm that separated the elite understanding of India from the 'real India'. Reconciling the difference between the elite understanding of India versus the real India is a conflict that persists even today.

As I met my fellow batchmates and other students at Hindu College (which was known to bring in a far more diverse crowd than many leading colleges of the university), I realized that my notions of merit, talent and ideology were all built on shaky foundations. Up sprung the question: what is the real India? I met friends who had come from not-so-well-off families, residing in the interiors of Bihar, do well in the IAS examination and contribute immensely to public service in India. Many others, from Maharashtra, Gujarat and lesser-known educational circles of the country, had remarkable ambition and motivation. Far removed from the homogeneity of the urban elite, their drive to excel and their 'independent' ideologies were a by-product of their lived experience and were moulded by the grammar of their traditions and cultures.

I am glad that I was a student at Hindu College. Its mission of imparting secular education, with a focus on creating vibrant spaces for scholarship, where frank and free dialogue was encouraged, made it a distinct centre for learning. It afforded us the opportunity to question dominant narratives of the time and study the sociopolitical affairs of the day from multiple independent lenses, not just through one set of red-tinted glasses (pun intended).

Most dominant narratives are axiomatically shaped by the maturity and strength of the intellectual discourse of the day. And the dominant narrative in my day was that of the

Left and Marxist institutions, which had hijacked the elite quotient of public debate and scholarship. The influences of Karl Marx as well as the different shades of socialism that Prime Minister Jawaharlal Nehru had imbibed after Independence came to define public discourse, despite its obviously ill-fitted contours with the pluralistic and civilizational nature of Indian life. Being a leading public space for debate, this dominance was largely observed in the university as well. There was a severe dichotomy within the Delhi University Students Union (DUSU)—sharply divided between the Left and the Right.

Prominent personalities of the university teaching faculty actively built 'the cadre' while promoting leftist schools of thought. They promoted students who were ideologically aligned for learning opportunities and scholastic events over other equally deserving candidates. It was surprising to me that these 'enlightened people', who were using historical materialism for analysis, were able to obfuscate the discourse so thoroughly through their doublespeak. For instance, they had voluble approval for their supportive stance on China's first nuclear test in October 1964—conveniently forgetting that the Sino-Indian war had happened only two years before that—even as they termed India's nuclear tests in May 1974 as 'irresponsible'. Their disdain for what is loosely termed as the Right permeated into the university pathos. It pushed away many students from publicly exploring their own cultures and knowledge systems for fear of being branded as a 'Sanghi'—the basest insult that one could receive in an intellectual reservoir such as DU.

One tragicomic incident comes to mind as I think of the bizarreness of the Left's intellectual heavy-handedness at the university. I was part of a student agitation in 1971 that had snowballed into a rather serious affair. It had resulted in the dean of student welfare, Mahender Singh, being in the crosshairs of the student community. Many slogans were raised against him personally during the agitation. I remember going into a discussion with him immediately after the agitation, fearing that we were all going to get rusticated. He, however, was more concerned with the personal nature of our sloganeering, brooding over some choice remarks made against him by some members of the Congress-affiliated National Students Union of India (NSUI), including: 'Mahender Singh kutta; Mahender Singh dalla; Mahender Singh Jan Sanghi.' It was not being called a dog or a pimp but a 'Sanghi' that stung him the most. That was what he couldn't take. Such was the subversion of the mind!

I had real-life brushes with the divergence around the Right and Left early in my life, though I would not fully appreciate the contours of that debate for many years to come. My father, an official in the Ministry of External Affairs (MEA), received orders for his first overseas posting to Belgrade. The year was 1957. Travel on posting was an enjoyable affair, which involved sea journey by a cruise liner. In this case, *MV Asia*, *Lloyd Triestino* from Bombay via Cairo Port, Suez Canal, Naples in Italy and then Genoa. When the ship reached Naples, a telegram was received from the MEA, redirecting my father to Bonn, the capital of the Federal Republic of

Germany, instead of Belgrade. It was not clear as to why this change had been affected. In most such cases, the bureaucracy invokes 'exigencies of service' as an explanation, when none is required to be given, then or now. The years in Bonn passed happily, and my first exposure to schooling was in a German kindergarten.

A few years later, back in the MEA, my father was to face another administrative hiccup. Being the man he was, he refused to make an issue, but my mother decided that his reticence did not prevent her from speaking to Mrs Badruddin Tyabji, whom she knew from our days in Bonn. Tyabji was the Indian ambassador to Germany between 1958 and 1960, after which he had returned to the MEA and was secretary in charge of administration.

A few days later, the whole story tumbled out, in the form of an old Intelligence Bureau (IB) report. It was based on a complaint filed by a school teacher against my grandfather Sardar Kartar Singh Puri, who was principal of a government school in Mehrauli, immediately after Partition. Apparently, my grandfather had fired this teacher for some reason or other. Wanting to get even, the school teacher had filed a complaint saying that the principal and his two sons—my father and his elder brother—were known 'communists'. Evidence cited was the fact that my grandfather subscribed to a newspaper called *Preet Lari*.

Many years later, when his granddaughters were told this story, they had a hearty laugh. They wondered how one could get it so wrong because he was a stickler for propriety, abided by the rule of law and had a view of the Raj that was different from someone with any left-wing leanings. In any case, the attempt to brand him 'leftist' ended up in him being posted to Bonn instead of Belgrade!

Later, this line of argument also helped resolve another mystery. My father's elder brother had been transferred from a sensitive desk in the defence ministry to one in the home ministry. I recall relating the story many years later with some batchmates who found their security clearance was being delayed, resulting in their joining the Academy in Mussoorie a few days late. I made it a point to peep into my own security clearance folder in my personal file when I became under-secretary (Foreign Service Personnel) in the MEA. I was amused to find that it contained a short summary of some of my debating speeches at DU supporting Bangladesh's liberation. While filing the report, the uninformed inspector or 'source' didn't realize that the two-member college team was usually divided into one speaking for the motion and the other, against it. If I had been asked to oppose the motion, I would have said exactly the opposite. That would have meant taking a position against the government. Would that have denied or delayed my security clearance? For anyone not familiar with the political ethos of the 1950s and 1960s, this represented, in a sense, only a resonance of the McCarthy phobia sweeping the world then: 'Look for the commie under the bed!' Of course, this would also have been sorted out eventually. In any case, this phobia was to drastically change in the 1970s when Left-of-Centre became the flavour of the season.

Even in college, I faced this 'stigma' when I was contesting for the post of college prime minister in the student parliament of Hindu College. Many within the student community thought that I was an avowed communist because I was one of Bipan Chandra's favourite students. Some in the Akhil Bharatiya Vidyarthi Parishad (ABVP) were initially hesitant to vote for me despite my professed Right-of-Centre stance on various political issues. It took all my skills of persuasion to convince many blocs in the student body that I did not espouse the Left view.

A Personal Intellectual Framework versus Continuing with a Colonial Mindset

The third conflict that I experienced at DU flows directly from the second conflict. When it became obvious to me and many other students that the 'real' India was being subverted by the Left elite, it was only natural that the dominant narrative would soon be challenged. The Left, misguided in their politics and support for various causes that were fundamentally distanced from the goings-on in India, strongly disavowed their own nationalism in favour of an entirely foreign value system. Filling in the intellectual vacuum left by the departing British, the Left viewpoint dominated discourse, starting in the early post-Independence years and ascending to the top of India's intellectually stratified society in the 1970s. While we had just overthrown political colonization and chosen a contrasting approach to redress economic colonialism, we continued to suffer from a different but equally insidious type of cultural and intellectual colonialism.

Despite institutions such as Jawaharlal Nehru University continuing to be dominated by various strands of leftist thought, DU was able to nurture healthy bastions of liberal and conservative thought. We questioned why the public discourse was being framed in an interpretation that contradicted oral and documented Indian history as well as methods that were alien to the values and interests of the majority of Indians. Accelerated by the Emergency and greater global interconnectedness in the decades to come, the Indian educational institution became a thriving space for the re-examination of the Left intellectual framework.

Within DU, an interesting exchange was ignited by Tapan Raychaudhuri's searching speculation of Morris D. Morris's thesis of reinterpreting colonial India's economic history in the nineteenth century. The thesis was also addressed by the likes of Bipan Chandra, Hitesranjan Sanyal and Toru Matsui in *The Indian Economic and Social History Review* (IESHR) in 1968. In a lengthy exchange, some key messages that Morris touched upon were his scepticism of the empire theory of underdevelopment and the criticism of the imperialist policy as the main factor behind India's lack of growth. He suggested that British India was among the poorest British colonies in the nineteenth century, and the State played the role of a passive actor, a 'night-watchman', which created enabling conditions for the private sector to flourish.

While I will leave it to the reader to explore Morris's

substantiation, I believe it is fair—if a little crude—to summarize that he argued for British rule, on balance. He asserted that British rule created a 'modern Indian state', which was based on institutions and an order that facilitated economic growth by integrating Indian commodities and labour with British capital and knowhow. This conveniently ignored the historical reality that India was among the richest and most well-connected economies in the world in the preceding centuries and was left impoverished, 'coincidentally', after 190 years of exploitative British rule.

Raychaudhuri and the rest challenged this viewpoint vigorously and contended that Morris's views soft-pedalled and even ignored the destructive colonial influence on the Indian economy and polity, and especially on indigenous entrepreneurship. I do not know how much illumination the debate provided and what consensus it was able to produce immediately, but the groundswell raised by the debate compelled many to reconsider the dominant interpretation of colonial history. In many other institutions across the country, a similar fire was being lit.

My own awakening happened in college, where I was shocked to see friends from across party lines espouse leftist/colonial language in their conversations, without critical thinking. Having been a student of history myself, I believe a good student is advised to ask 'who is the historian', what are his/her biases, how much of what has been written is 'commissioned', and if the account is borne out by objective reality recorded elsewhere. The horrors of British rule were prevalent and accessible, and yet they were couched in revisionist and ambivalent terms by many leading historians, including some prominent Indians.

Despite the unpopularity it could have brought me, I was among the first students in my generation to question why the dominant narrative was accepted without question. This conflict finds even more resonance today in the evolving global order of the twenty-first century. The intellectual subjugation has sunk in deep—it is a battle to reclaim Indian self-esteem that we are still fighting.

Since the early 1970s, many events in India's sociopolitical journey have been marked by important decolonizing milestones, the most salient of which, I believe, was the unprecedented mandate given to Prime Minister Narendra Modi, in May 2014, of establishing a distinct Indian identity. In the eight years since, large-scale social and financial inclusion underpinned by the government's philosophy of *Sabka Saath, Sabka Vikas, Sabka Vishwas, Sabka Prayas* has resulted in the emergence of 'a new India'. The Modi government has defied the 'Right-Left' labelling altogether and is developing a new Indian spirit that fuses the modern with the civilizational. The objective of delivering services to the farthest first, captured in the core tenet of *Antyodaya se Sarvodaya*, is not only a governance paradigm that aims to do away with social stratification but also a winning formula to meet the targets of India's Sustainable Development Goals (SDGs).

As I was leaving DU to join the IFS, it struck me that I was putting aside an intellectual framework that I knew was riddled with gaps in favour of a personal methodology that was as yet amorphous. This new approach was based on first principles from which I could reason and deliberate, and form my own perspective of events. That, I think, was the true distinction of my university graduation. It taught me how to discern.

University education, equally within textbooks as much without, imparted inquisitiveness and the ability to discern and dissect. It also exposed reality and its contradictions in many unsettling ways. It was hard to see that your nation wasn't as united as you thought it was, or your heroes weren't as perfect as you thought they were, or issues weren't as clear-cut as they were. University education gave me the opportunity to build on foundational principles and develop a consistent value system. Knowledge went far beyond ideas and patents. I am reminded of that George Bernard Shaw saying, which feels apt in this moment: 'A fool's brain digests philosophy into folly, science into superstition, and art into pedantry. Hence university education.'

Would I have been able to achieve the same education elsewhere? Would colleges in Punjab, or others in Delhi, or even abroad, such as Oxford and Cambridge, have been able to equip me with the education that I not just sought but also needed? I think not. Certainly, the trajectory of my intellectual growth would have been different had I studied in an Oxbridge college, but it would have failed to expose me to the reality of the human condition as well as the lived experience of millions of Indians. I am sure that the range and depth of personal development that I acquired at DU could not have been matched anywhere else, for the simple reason that it was a unique time in the evolution of Delhi and the various institutions and ideals that built modern India. One had to be there to absorb the heady cocktail of charged political discourse, rich cultural exchange and volatile socio-economic trends. It forced us to 'grow up' in ways that the comforts of other academic settings would not have been able to provide.

I realized how quickly I had shed my innocence in college. I had many mentors who, true to the DU spirit, were always there to guide me towards the right path. Suresh Sapra, who was college prime minister a couple of years before me, helped me navigate the nuances of student political life. Ashok Mittal—who has been associated with the university for almost 60 years and is now part of the governing council—was not only a lecturer when I was studying at Hindu College but also a confidant, advocate and constant supporter throughout. Their influence ensured I steered clear of many morally suspect trends at the time, foremost among which were Naxalism and drugs. Of course, college life in the late 1960s and early 1970s meant that dalliances with pot and a lifelong love for Pink Floyd were all par for the course. Ashok's guidance was not just to do with the 'rough and tumble' of college and hostel life but also about how we had to become hardened to deal with the world.

Inbuilt in the evolution of my worldview was a healthy scepticism of the dominant narrative. I realized that as one of the many privileged young Indians who had inherited a new India in the aftermath of the Emergency, it was incumbent upon me to let go of imposed mindsets and think about matters of public or national importance with originality. I would like to think that an entire generation thought like that. Despite the obvious shortcomings of the job market, we were determined to carry on the legacy of the independence movement and the national struggle during the Emergency.

The previous generation had laid down the blueprint for the safeguarding of national unity and the pursuit of national goals. It was our job to take that forward and give wings to the national spirit.

ABOUT THE CONTRIBUTORS

Imtiaz Ali (Hindu College, 1990–93) is a director, writer and producer. Some of his critically acclaimed films include *Socha Na Tha* (2005), *Jab We Met* (2007), *Love Aaj Kal* (2009) and *Rockstar* (2011). He is also the writer and creator of *She* (Season 2), a web series streaming on Netflix. He is a founder member of Ibtida, the dramatics society of Hindu College (still in progress).

Justice (Dr) Dhananjaya Y. Chandrachud (St. Stephen's College, 1976–79; Campus Law Centre 1979–82) is a judge of the Supreme Court of India. Before this, he was the Chief Justice of the Allahabad High Court (October 2013–May 2016). He was a judge of the Bombay High Court for 13 years (March 2000–October 2013). Justice Chandrachud joined the Bombay Bar after obtaining LLM and SJD degrees from Harvard Law School. He was designated as a senior advocate in June 1998 and served as Additional Solicitor General of India.

Dr Bibek Debroy (Delhi School of Economics, 1974–76) is chairman of the Economic Advisory Council to the Prime Minister. He has worked in universities, research institutions, chambers and government (prior to the present assignment), including as member of NITI Aayog (2015–17). He has published several books and writes popular articles for newspapers/magazines. He also translates texts from Sanskrit to English and has the unusual distinction of honorary doctorates in both economics and Sanskrit.

Namita Gokhale (Jesus and Mary College, 1973–did not complete) is the author of 20 works of fiction and non-fiction, and a Sahitya Akademi (National Academy of Letters) awardee for 2021. She is co-founder and co-director of the Jaipur Literature Festival. Gokhale was conferred the prestigious First Centenary National Award for Literature by the Asam Sahitya Sabha in 2017, and has received recognition both for her writing and her commitment to multilingual Indian literature and cross-cultural literary dialogue.

Image courtesy: Mayank Austen Soofi

Dr Meenakshi Gopinath ((Lady Shri Ram College, 1966–69; and as faculty, 1974–88, and principal, 1988–2014)) is currently chair, Centre for Policy Research, and founder-director of Women in Security, Conflict Management and Peace (WISCOMP). She is also principal emerita of Lady Shri Ram College, an association of nearly five decades. A member of multitrack peace initiatives, her work and publications focus on gender, security, peacebuilding and education. She has received national and international awards for her contribution to the field of education, including the Padma Shri. She was the first woman to serve on the National Security Advisory Board of India.

Arnab Goswami (Hindu College, 1990–93) is the editor-in-chief, founder and owner of the Republic Media Network. Goswami holds a bachelor's degree in sociology, and was a Felix Scholar at Oxford and a fellow at Cambridge University. A first-generation news entrepreneur, Goswami is India's leading TV anchor and president of the News Broadcasters Federation. He strongly believes in free-market economics, which he advocates in his approach to the media space as well.

Raian Karanjawala (Shri Ram College of Commerce, 1972–75) is managing partner at Karanjawala & Co. Among its many achievements and accolades, his firm is a recipient of approximately 180 awards for Best Litigation Firm. Karanjawala was also named one of the 50 most influential people in India by *India Today* magazine in 2004. He was awarded the Degree of an Honorary Doctor of Laws (LL.D) by Amity University in 2014.

Hardeep S. Puri (Hindu College, 1968–73; Lecturer, St. Stephen's College 1973–74) is Union Minister of housing and urban affairs, and minister of petroleum and natural gas. He had a distinguished four-decade career in diplomacy, spanning the bilateral and multilateral arena, having held ambassadorial posts in London and Brasilia, and as permanent representative of India to the United Nations in both Geneva (2002–05) and New York (2009–13). He is one of the few Indians to have presided over the United Nations Security Council and the first to have chaired its Counter-Terrorism Committee.

Lakshmi Puri (Lady Shri Ram College, 1970–73) was the youngest entrant into the Indian Foreign Service at the age of 21 and served as ambassador to Hungary. After representing India abroad in key bilateral and multilateral diplomatic assignments for 28 years, she served at the United Nations for 15 years in various capacities, where she contributed to the humanities' projects of peace and security, sustainable development and climate change, human rights and humanitarian action. She is a Distinguished Fellow of the Indian Association of International Studies (IAIS) and recipient of the prestigious Eleanor Roosevelt Prize for Human Rights, among others.

Kiren Rijiju (Hansraj College, 1986–89; Faculty of Law, 1989–94) is the Union Minister of law and justice, and Member of Parliament from Arunachal West. He has successfully established himself as the face and voice of Northeast India. Owing to his outstanding contribution as a parliamentarian, he was duly adjudged 'The Best Young Parliamentarian' by the media. He is also the first Indian to be designated as Disaster Risk Champion for the Asia Pacific Region by the United Nations due to his work in the area of disaster management.

Sanjeev Sanyal (Shri Ram College of Commerce, 1989–92) is currently a member of the Economic Advisory Council to the Prime Minister. He was the principal economic adviser to the finance minister for five years till February 2022 and the co-chair of the G20's Framework Working Group. Sanyal attended Oxford University as a Rhodes Scholar. He was awarded the Eisenhower Fellowship in 2007 for his work on urban dynamics. In 2010, he was named as a Young Global Leader by the World Economic Forum in Davos. Sanyal is the author of a number of bestselling books and over 200 articles and columns in leading national and international publications.

Vijay Shekhar Sharma (Delhi College of Engineering, 1994–98) is a technology entrepreneur who has played an instrumental role in revolutionizing the digital payments and financial services landscape in India as the chairman, managing director and CEO of One97 Communications and its consumer brand Paytm. He has featured in the 2017 'Time 100' list of *Time* magazine. Sharma has also been bestowed with multiple industry honours—'Entrepreneur of the Year' award in 2018 by All India Management Association, 'Entrepreneur of the Year' at ET Awards for Corporate Excellence in 2016, and 'GQ Man of the Year' in 2016.

Prof. (Dr) Dinesh Singh (St. Stephen's College, 1972–78) has served as the twenty-first vice chancellor of Delhi University during 2010–15. He has been awarded the Padma Shri and several honorary doctorates from highly ranked institutions in Europe, the US and India for his work as a mathematician and an educationist. He holds an AICTE Distinguished Chair Professorship and is an adjunct professor of mathematics at the University of Houston, Texas, USA. He also serves as the chancellor of the K.R. Mangalam University.

Dr Shashi Tharoor (St. Stephen's College, 1972–75), a third-term Member of Parliament from Thiruvananthapuram, is the bestselling author of 22 books, both fiction and non-fiction, besides being a former under-secretary-general of the United Nations and a former minister of state for human resource development and for external affairs. He is the recipient of numerous awards, including the Pravasi Bharatiya Samman, a Commonwealth Writers' Prize and the Crossword Lifetime Achievement Award. In 2019, Tharoor was also awarded the Sahitya Akademi Award in the category of 'English Non-Fiction' for his book *An Era of Darkness*. He chairs Parliament's Standing Committee on Information Technology.